Anonymous

Celebration of the Fiftieth Anniversary of the Appointment of Professor William Henry Green

As An Instructor in Princeton Theological Seminary

Anonymous

Celebration of the Fiftieth Anniversary of the Appointment of Professor William Henry Green

As An Instructor in Princeton Theological Seminary

ISBN/EAN: 9783337169114

Printed in Europe, USA, Canada, Australia, Japan

Cover: Foto ©ninafisch / pixelio.de

More available books at **www.hansebooks.com**

TABLE OF CONTENTS

	PAGE
INTRODUCTION,	1

ADDRESSES

Dr. Gosman's Address,	16
Dr. Mead's Address,	20
Dr. McCurdy's Address,	31
Dr. Patton's Address,	37
Dr. Green's Reply,	44

CONGRATULATORY ADDRESSES

From the Presbyterian Church in the United States of America, by Dr. Booth,	51
From Our Sister Churches, by Dr. McPheeters,	53
From Our Sister Seminaries, by Dr. Beecher,	56
From Dr. Green's Alma Mater, by Dr. Warfield,	57
From the Trustees of Princeton College, by Dr. Alexander,	59
From the Old Testament Revision Committee, by Dr. Osgood,	60

AFTER-DINNER SPEECHES

The "Father of the Man," by Dr. Cattell,	65
Our Fellow-Student, by Dr. Cuyler,	68
The Young Professor, by Dr. Taylor,	72

TABLE OF CONTENTS

	PAGE
The Established Teacher, by Dr. Griffin,	76
The Learned Doctor, by Dr. Fox,	80
The Head of the Faculty, by Professor Paxton,	84

APPENDIX

TESTIMONIALS AND LETTERS OF REGRET

From Institutions of Learning and Associations,	89
From Individuals,	132
Press Articles,	156
BIBLIOGRAPHY,	181

INTRODUCTORY ACCOUNT

At a meeting of the Board of Directors of Princeton Theological Seminary, held in Princeton, October 8, 1895, the following action was taken :

"The Board of Directors, calling to mind the fact that this Seminary year will complete the period of a half-century since the appointment of Dr. William Henry Green as an Instructor in this institution, therefore, in view of the pre-eminently valuable and protracted services which Dr. Green, in the providence of God, has been enabled to render as an Instructor and Professor in this institution, the Board deem it due to Dr. Green, to ourselves, and to the cause of truth that some suitable and proper official and public recognition of the same should be had at the proper time, the close of this Seminary year, the fiftieth anniversary of his appointment. Therefore,

Resolved, That a Committee of five members of this Board, consisting of three ministers and two laymen, be appointed, with power, in co-operation with a Committee of the Trustees, a Committee of the Faculty, and the Executive Committee of the Alumni Association of the Seminary, to make all needful arrangements for such anniversary services."

In accordance with this resolution, the following Committee of the Board of Directors was appointed: the Rev. Ebenezer Erskine, D.D., Chairman, the Rev. George D. Baker, D.D., the Rev. Robert R. Booth, D.D., LL.D., George Junkin, LL.D., and Logan C. Murray, Esq.; and the Secretary of the Board was directed to send copies of the above action to the Board of Trustees, to the Faculty, and to the Executive Committee of the Alumni Association. On the 15th of October the Faculty appointed as the Committee called for by the action of the Directors, Professors B. B. Warfield, D.D., LL.D., John D. Davis, Ph.D., and George T. Purves, D.D., LL.D. The Trustees, at their meeting held on October 30th, appointed to represent them the Rev. Abraham Gosman, D.D., the Rev. John D. Wells, D.D., and the Rev. Edward B. Hodge, D.D.

On the 12th of November the Executive Committee of the Alumni Association, consisting of the Rev. William E. Schenck, D.D., the Rev. John Fox, D.D., the Rev. Joseph H. Dulles, the Rev. W. Brenton Greene, D.D., the Rev. Samuel J. Milliken, the Rev. Benjamin S. Everitt, D.D., and the Rev. Newell W. Wells, held a meeting and resolved to recommend to the Association that in view of the celebration of the fiftieth anniversary of Professor Green's connection with the Seminary as an Instructor, the Association consume only so much time at its annual meeting as is necessary for the election of officers for the ensuing year and the hearing of the customary reports.

The General Committee, composed of the several committees of the Board of Directors, the Board of Trustees, and the Executive Committee of the Alumni Association, met in Alexander Hall, November 12, 1895. The Rev. Dr. Gosman was elected Chairman and the Rev. B. S. Everitt, D.D., Secretary. A general outline of the programme for the celebration, to take place on Commencement Day, May 5, 1896, was adopted. This was afterward modified in some slight particulars. Dr. Erskine, together with the Committee of the Faculty, was made a Committee of Arrangements to perfect the programme. A Committee on Invitations was appointed, consisting of the Rev. Joseph H. Dulles, Professor Warfield, Dean J. O. Murray, the Rev. Newell W. Wells, and the Rev. Howard Duffield, D.D. The following were appointed a Committee on Finance: George Junkin, LL.D., the Rev. R. R. Booth, D.D., LL.D., and the Rev. E. B. Hodge, D.D. The Trustees present were requested to call the attention of the Board of Trustees to the desirability of securing a further endowment of the Seminary in connection with the celebration of the semi-centennial of Dr. Green's services. The Rev. Chalmers Martin was later added to the General Committee, to take charge of the entertainment of specially invited guests.

Through the labors of the above committees the arrangements for the celebration were completed. One change of moment in the programme was occasioned by the lamented death of the Rev. Talbot W. Chambers, D.D., LL.D., who had accepted the appointment to make one of the principal addresses, that upon Dr. Green's services to the Church at large. President Patton, of Princeton College, consented to take his place, as will hereafter appear. An invitation in the following form was sent the officers of the Seminary, to its living benefactors, to its alumni, to American Semitic scholars, to the theological institutions of this country, as well as to the more closely affiliated colleges, and to the theological faculties of Europe:

THE THEOLOGICAL SEMINARY OF THE
PRESBYTERIAN CHURCH IN THE UNITED STATES OF AMERICA,
AT PRINCETON, NEW JERSEY,
REQUESTS THE HONOR OF YOUR PRESENCE
ON TUESDAY, MAY THE FIFTH,
EIGHTEEN HUNDRED AND NINETY-SIX,
AT THE CELEBRATION OF THE FIFTIETH ANNIVERSARY
OF THE APPOINTMENT OF
PROFESSOR WILLIAM HENRY GREEN
AS AN INSTRUCTOR IN THE SEMINARY.

The replies received indicated a very widespread and warm interest in the celebration. Many of the letters of regret from institutions that could not send a representative and from individuals who could not attend will be found published at the close of this volume.

What may well be termed the most notable Commencement Day in the history of the Seminary began with the usual graduation exercises in Miller Chapel. These were followed by a brief meeting of the Alumni Association. Upon its adjournment a procession was formed in the Seminary campus under the marshalship of Professor William Libbey, of the College, and marched in the following order to Alexander Hall, on the College campus, which was kindly put at the disposition of the Committee by the College authorities:

> Presiding Officers
> Representatives of other Institutions
> Directors of the Seminary
> Trustees of the Seminary
> Speakers of the Day
> Faculty of the Seminary
> Trustees and Faculty of the College
> Invited Guests
> Alumni of the Seminary by Classes
> Graduating Class
> Undergraduates.

Dr. Green met the procession in Alexander Hall, which was filled to its utmost capacity. The programme that follows was successfully carried out. There was found to be no time to read the selected letters of regret received from institutions and individuals. Instead of this, Dr. Schenck made a few remarks with reference to the number and warmth of these letters and Dean Murray made the announcement, which was received with much enthusiasm, that it was proposed to mark the completion of Dr. Green's fifty years' services in an enduring way by the raising of one hundred thousand dollars for the endowment of a William Henry Green Memorial Professorship of Semitic Languages.

PRINCETON THEOLOGICAL SEMINARY
EIGHTY FOURTH ANNUAL COMMENCEMENT.

FIFTIETH ANNIVERSARY
OF THE APPOINTMENT OF
PROFESSOR WILLIAM HENRY GREEN, D.D., LL.D.
AS INSTRUCTOR IN THE SEMINARY
TUESDAY MAY 5TH 1896.

Jubilee Celebration

ALEXANDER HALL, AT ELEVEN O'CLOCK A.M.
Presided over by the President of the Board of Directors.

HYMN . . . . "I LOVE THY KINGDOM, LORD."

PRAYER . . . . THE REV. JOHN GULIAN LANSING, D.D.
Professor in the Theological Seminary of the Reformed Church in America,
at New Brunswick

Opening Address

DR. GREEN'S SERVICES TO THE SEMINARY . THE REV. ABRAHAM GOSMAN, D.D.
President of the Board of Directors

Addresses

DR. GREEN'S CONTRIBUTION TO BIBLICAL CRITICISM
THE REV. CHARLES M. MEAD, PH.D., D.D.
Riley Professor of Christian Theology, Hartford Theological Seminary

DR. GREEN'S CONTRIBUTION TO SEMITIC SCHOLARSHIP
THE REV. J. F. MCCURDY, PH.D., LL.D.
Professor of Oriental Literature, University College, Toronto

DR. GREEN'S SERVICES TO THE CHURCH AT LARGE
THE REV. FRANCIS L. PATTON, D.D., LL.D.
President of Princeton College

Reply by Professor Green

Congratulatory Addresses

FROM

THE PRESBYTERIAN CHURCH IN THE U. S. A.
THE REV. ROBERT RUSSELL BOOTH, D.D., LL.D.
Moderator of the General Assembly

OUR SISTER CHURCHES . . . . THE REV. WM. M. MCPHEETERS, D.D.
Professor in Columbia Theological Seminary

OUR SISTER SEMINARIES . . . . THE REV. WILLIS J. BEECHER, D.D.
Professor in Auburn Theological Seminary

DR. GREEN'S "ALMA MATER" . . . . . ETHELBERT DUDLEY WARFIELD, LL.D.
President of Lafayette College

THE TRUSTEES OF PRINCETON COLLEGE . . HENRY M. ALEXANDER, LL.D.
New York City

THE OLD TESTAMENT REVISION COMMITTEE
THE REV. HOWARD OSGOOD, D.D., LL.D.
Professor in Rochester Theological Seminary

Replies to Invitations

READ BY THE REV. WM. E. SCHENCK, D.D. . . . Secretary of the Board of Directors

HYMN . . . . "OUR GOD STANDS FIRM, A ROCK AND TOW'R."

Benediction

BY THE REV. JOHN H. MUNRO, D.D. Pastor of the Central Presbyterian Church, Phila.

Alumni Dinner

UNIVERSITY HALL, AT TWO O'CLOCK P.M.

PRESIDED OVER BY THE REV. WILLIAM E. SCHENCK, D.D.
President of the Alumni Association

BLESSING ASKED BY THE REV. ADOLPH SPAETH, D.D., Professor in the Lutheran Theological Seminary, at Philadelphia, Pa.

Reminiscence Meeting

ALEXANDER HALL, AT THREE O'CLOCK P.M.
DR. SCHENCK PRESIDING.

Toasts

THE "FATHER OF THE MAN"
THE REV. WILLIAM C. CATTELL, D.D., LL.D., Class of 1852
Sometime President of Lafayette College ; Corresponding Secretary of the Board of Ministerial Relief

OUR FELLOW STUDENT . . . THE REV. THEODORE L. CUYLER, D.D., Class of 1846
Sometime Pastor of the Lafayette Avenue Presbyterian Church, Brooklyn, N. Y.

THE YOUNG PROFESSOR . . . THE REV. A. A. E. TAYLOR, D.D., LL.D., Class of 1857
Pastor of the Westminster Presbyterian Church, Columbus, O.

THE ESTABLISHED TEACHER
THE REV. EDWARD H. GRIFFIN, D.D., LL.D., Class of 1866
Dean of the Johns Hopkins University

THE LEARNED DOCTOR . . . . THE REV. JOHN FOX, D.D., Class of 1876
Pastor of the Second Presbyterian Church, Brooklyn, N. Y.

THE HEAD OF THE FACULTY
THE REV. WILLIAM M. PAXTON, D.D., LL.D., Class of 1848
Professor in Princeton Seminary

Benediction

BY CANON ARTHUR J. MASON, D.D., Lady Margaret Professor of Divinity in Cambridge University, England

At the close of the public exercises Professor and Mrs. Green gave a reception at their home, on Stockton Street, which was largely attended.

The following institutions were represented at the celebration :

The theological faculty of the University of Cambridge, England, by Canon A. J. Mason, D.D.; the theological faculty of Trinity College, Dublin, by Rev. John Hall, D.D., LL.D., of New York City; Princeton College, by the clerical members of its faculty; Auburn Theological Seminary, by Professor Willis J. Beecher, D.D.; McCormick Theological Seminary, by Professor Andrew C. Zenos, D.D.; German Theological Seminary of Newark, N. J., by President Charles E. Knox, D.D.; Lincoln University, by Professors J. Aspinwall Hodge, D.D., and William D. Kerswill, A.M.; Omaha Theological Seminary, by Professor William W. Harsha, D.D., LL.D.; Western Theological Seminary, by Professor Robert D. Wilson, D.D.; Columbia Theological Seminary, by Professor Wm. M. McPheeters, D.D.; Yale Divinity School, by Professor George P. Fisher, D.D., LL.D.; Harvard Divinity School, by Professor Crawford H. Toy, D.D.; Andover Theological Seminary, by Professor George F. Moore, D.D.; Hartford Theological Seminary, by Professor Charles M. Mead, Ph.D., D.D.; University of Chicago, by President William R. Harper, D.D., LL.D.; University of Pennsylvania, by Provost C. C. Harrison, LL.D.; Rochester Theological Seminary, by Professor Howard Osgood, D.D., LL.D.; Crozer Theological Seminary, by Professor B. C. Taylor, D.D.; Xenia Theological Seminary, by Professor David MacDill, D.D.; Theological Department of Howard University, by Dean J. S. Ewell, D.D.; Baptist Theological Seminary, Louisville, Ky., by President W. H. Whitsitt, D.D.; Hamilton Theological Seminary, by Professor William H. Maynard, D.D.; Meadville Theological School (Unitarian), by Rev. Joseph May, LL.D.; Theological Seminary of the Evangelical Lutheran Church in Philadelphia, by Professors Adolph Spaeth, D.D., and George F. Spieker, Ph.D., D.D.; Rutgers College, by Professors Jacob Cooper, S.T.D., D.C.L., John H. Duryea, D.D., and Charles E. Hart, D.D.; Seminary of the Reformed

Church in America at New Brunswick, N. J., by Professor Samuel M. Woodbridge, D.D., LL.D.; Amherst College, by Professor H. H. Neill; Theological Seminary of the Evangelical Lutheran Church at Chicago, by President R. F. Weidner, D.D., LL.D.; General Theological Seminary of the Protestant Episcopal Church, by Dean Eugene A. Hoffman, D.D., D.C.L., LL.D.; Department of Theology in Oberlin College, by Professor G. Frederic Wright, D.D., LL.D.; Protestant Episcopal Theological Seminary of Virginia, by Professor Angus Crawford, D.D.; Theological Seminary of the Reformed Church at Lancaster, Pa., by Professor F. A. Gast, D.D.; Lafayette College, by President Ethelbert D. Warfield, LL.D., Rev. William C. Cattell, D.D., LL.D., and George Junkin, LL.D.

The following brief sketch of Professor Green's life is taken from the *Princeton Press* of May 9, 1896:

William Henry Green was born at Groveville, near Princeton, January 27, 1825. He is a descendant of Jonathan Dickinson, the first President of Princeton College. His father was a successful merchant. One of his uncles was Chancellor of New Jersey and another was Judge of the Court of Errors and Appeals. The eldest of his father's brothers was the late John C. Green, of New York City, to whose princely benefactions during his lifetime and his munificent bequests the College, the Seminary, and the Lawrenceville School are so largely indebted for buildings and endowments. Dr. Green was graduated with honors at Lafayette College before he was sixteen years old, and immediately upon his graduation was made a tutor, and held that position for two years. He then entered the Princeton Theological Seminary in 1842, and remained there for a year, when Lafayette recalled him to the position of Instructor in Mathematics. After a year's service he returned to the Seminary, completed his course, and was graduated in 1846. The same year he was appointed Instructor in Hebrew in the Seminary. He has remained in this department from that date to the present with the exception of two years, 1849-51, when he was pastor of the Central Presbyterian Church,

Philadelphia. His literary labors, aside from the duties of his professorship, have been abundant.* Scores of articles in the *Biblical Repertory*, the *Princeton* and *Presbyterian Reviews*, and other journals have been written by him, for the most part on Old Testament and philological subjects. His published volumes include his Hebrew Grammar, "The Pentateuch Vindicated from the Aspersions of Bishop Colenso," "Hebrew Chrestomathy," "Elementary Hebrew Grammar," "The Song of Solomon" in Lange's Commentary, "The Book of Job Unfolded," "Moses and the Prophets," "The Hebrew Feasts," "The Higher Criticism of the Pentateuch," and "The Unity of the Book of Genesis."

After the resignation of Dr. John Maclean, in 1868, he was elected President of Princeton College, but declined. He was the Chairman of the Old Testament Section of the American Bible Revision Committee, and was Moderator of the Presbyterian General Assembly in 1891. His degree of doctor of divinity was conferred upon him by Princeton College in 1857, and by the University of Edinburgh in 1884. His degree of doctor of laws he received from Rutgers College in 1873. Standing as one of the foremost Old Testament scholars, Dr. Green has also been eminently successful as an instructor, and has won the affection of all his students by his modest, unassuming and sympathetic personality.

* For a complete bibliography see the close of this volume.

OPENING PRAYER AND ADDRESSES

PRAYER

BY THE REV. PROFESSOR JOHN GULIAN LANSING, D.D.

Above the thrice holy cry of the Seraphim, Thou delightest to hear the praises and prayers of Thy children, O Lord God Almighty. We praise Thee because Thou art our Covenant Jehovah. We praise Thee because of Thy goodness, which is great, and Thy loving kindnesses, which have endured forever. We praise Thee because Thou art our Good Shepherd, leading us into the pastures of Thy love and by the waters still as Thine own deep peace. We praise Thee especially because Thou hast brought us to this day wherein we celebrate the long-continued and faithful usefulness of Thy servant.

We praise Thee because Thou hast given this Thy servant to this place, and this State, and this land, and this world. We praise Thee for all that he has been enabled to do through the Spirit of Jehovah resting upon him. We praise Thee for what he has done in Thy service in the interpretation, the defence, and the proclamation of divine truth. We praise Thee because Thou hast so continued his life and filled his life with blessings, and, through his life, blessed others. We thank Thee that through his instruction Thou hast given many the knowledge of the Word, who have gone forth to proclaim that Word throughout the world. We pray Thee, our Heavenly Father, that Thou will continue his life of usefulness unto us, and unto Thy Church, and unto those whom he equips for blessed usefulness in the field of the world. Grant to him, we beseech of Thee, all the blessings that come from Father, Son, and Holy Spirit. Let there evermore rest upon him the spirit of wisdom and understanding, the spirit of counsel and of might, the spirit of knowledge and of the fear of Jehovah. We ask it all for Thy name's sake. Amen.

DR. GREEN'S SERVICES TO THE SEMINARY.

BY THE REV. ABRAHAM GOSMAN, D.D.

My dear Dr. Green:

In the name of the Directors and Trustees, I welcome you to this fiftieth anniversary of your office and work in this Seminary. We may well congratulate any one whose life-work is so nearly rounded and complete; who can look upon the product of his toil and say, not without regrets as to his failures and a painful consciousness that it comes far short of his own ideal, yet with a large measure of truth, and with entire reverence, " It is finished." It was a wise act when the General Assembly selected you for this chair, which you have filled with such conspicuous success, and we rejoice with you to-day in the mellowed fruits which we have gathered and in the promise which greets us when the autumn sun shall have ripened those not yet fully matured.

To train those who are to preach the Gospel: there is no higher office and none more fruitful or wide-reaching in its influence. Our Lord Jesus Himself devoted a large part of His ministerial life to this end. He taught the multitude, but it was the inner circle of the Twelve, to whom He unfolded the mysteries of His kingdom. He brought them into the closest relation to Himself, and was ever training them for their great work. This was the first theological seminary, and they were highly favored who sat in its seats and listened to the Great Teacher. He opened to them the Scriptures. He ever found the germs and roots of his doctrine in the Old Testament Scriptures, and thus set his seal upon their inspiration. He believed in Moses, as you believe in him and have given us such good reason for your faith. He trained them in the Word and in the method of His service, and in this teaching laid the foundation of His kingdom. It was a most practical theology, as all true theological teaching is and must be. For it deals with those truths which are the great moving force in the hearts and lives of men, which stir most deeply all the fountains of Christian feeling, which strengthen all the motives to Christian activity and effort, which keep aflame the life of devotion and love, and yield their fruit unto holiness. This most effective and fruitful life has been yours, and we rejoice, therefore, in the success which crowns your life-work to-day. May I say it is a rare and unsullied crown which you so fitly wear?

Your service here stands closely related to the Seminary itself in its individual life and history. Every institution like this has its specific life and character, more or less distinctly marked, known and read of all men. It shares in the common life of the Church and has its individual features shaped somewhat by the circumstances in which it had its origin, somewhat by its surroundings in the line of its progress, but chiefly by the men who have taught here. It has never sought unduly to assert itself, but neither has it shunned the call which the interests of the truth and the kingdom of Christ have made. It has studied the peace and quiet of the Church, but not by the sacrifice of its faith. It has let its moderation be known to all men, but has never wavered in its adherence to the truth. It stands by the inspired Word of God in its completeness, the only norm of its faith and teaching. It holds with unwavering confidence the system of truth it finds in the Word, but has never claimed that there must be an iron rigidity in every form of expression or in every particular feature the truth wears. It recognizes that in the progress of Christian learning, in the growing acquaintance with oriental modes of thought, in the wider experience of believers, and especially in the larger gifts of the Holy Spirit, there is reason to hope that greater light may be thrown upon the Word and the Church come into the fuller possession of its heritage. It waits for that fuller light with supreme confidence as to the issue. It makes no boastful claim to any exclusive possession of the truth. It gladly recognizes that there are other institutions standing along the same line and sharing its responsibilities. But it does claim that it stands for Christ and the truth, the incarnate and the written Word. Its history fully vindicates its claim. In the conflict between faith and unbelief it has never given an uncertain sound. This is its crown of glory, this gives it its individual life and character, recognized alike by friends and foes.

Now, it is a grand thing, surely, to contribute in any measure to the fulness and richness of that life. Hence we come to-day, and with thankfulness to God, who gave you to us, we recognize your great service to this institution, as you have taken up the reins which have fallen into your hands from the illustrious men who have gone before you, and have guided it in its course and work through trials and perils and vigorous controversy, so that now, with its full and admirable equipment and a steadfast reliance upon God, it goes with a clear eye, a strong hand, and steady step to its work in the future for Christ, for the Word of God, and for the redemption of the world.

But this direct service to the Seminary lies within comparatively narrow limits. It cannot be separated from its wider sphere in those who have gone out into the field, moved, impelled, and qualified here for their work. If we would see the teacher in his true character and service, we must see him not as he is in the seclusion of the study, or in the class-room, not merely in the fruits of his pen, but in the ever widening circle of those who have been with him and learned of him. The vast mountain peak which stands out clearly defined upon the distant horizon impresses us as we look upon it; it grows in our conception of its size and power, but we get no adequate apprehension of it, we form no accurate judgment of its magnificence until we see it encircled by peaks of greater or less prominence, all clothed with forest and verdure and beauty, as their roots strike into the broad plain upon which all are based; nor do the streams which come from the central mount lose their sweetness and healthfulness, though tinged, it may be, by the soil through which they have passed. As we look upon those who have gone out from this institution into the wide field of the world, men of every grade of culture and power, but all men of faith and prayer, we begin to see, we only begin—the full results are not reached with the lapse of fifty years—we begin to see what the service of that man must be who stimulates and strengthens and guides them in their course. We see the teacher in the men of faith and power whom he has trained. The life of the Seminary comes to its richest fruitage in the works which these men have wrought. They have not been idlers or mere spectators in the world's progress. There is scarcely a line of human thought or energy in which they have not risen to distinction. They have been a mighty factor in all that is true and good. They have explored and cultivated and widened new fields of human knowledge. They have enriched the world's literature by their contributions. They have been pioneers. Human tongues have been reduced to writing, and great races have been started on the lines of progress, to whose mighty tread the world has not yet ceased to listen. Civilization follows in the wake of their toil. Science owes a large debt to their contributions. And to-day the Seminary rejoices in their power, their usefulness, and their promise.

It would be an easy and a grateful task to trace all this fruitage, in large part at least, to the influence and tireless toil of their teacher. But now we turn from the works of others and take up our Hebrew grammar, with its roots, inflexions, and syntax; we walk with Job in the furnace of trial, and share in his vindication and the triumph of his faith and patience; we sit down as invited guests at the Hebrew feasts in their historical and typical import; we open our Pentateuch as it comes to us out of the fires of criticism, and are sure that we have it as Moses gave it to us, as it has lived and shaped the faith of the ages, as it bears the seal of Christ Himself, and without the smell of fire upon it. With these fruits of your toil in our hands, and with a heartfelt satisfaction in your fifty years of successful toil which we cannot express, and a consciousness of our indebtedness which we can never repay, we say, Welcome, dear and honored Sir; thanks, beloved Teacher and Friend.

DR. GREEN'S CONTRIBUTION TO BIBLICAL CRITICISM.

BY THE REV. PROFESSOR CHARLES M. MEAD, D.D.

A GERMAN adage says, "Jubiläen sind Ululäen," which may be freely rendered, "Jubilations are tribulations." That is to say, the man whose Jubilee others most gladly celebrate may well be one who is so keenly aware of his shortcomings that the commendations given seem undeserved, and therefore painful. To be praised to one's face is an ordeal which can be passed through without embarrassment only by one who is so self-satisfied that he had better not be praised at all. What then? Shall we now put a seal on our lips, lest we offend the modesty of him on whose account we have come together? Nay, verily; for our part is to commemorate services for which the Christian public has occasion to be grateful. We must judge for ourselves whether we are warranted in doing so; and if he who has rendered the services deprecates the praise, we will praise him all the more for the modesty which deprecates it.

It falls to me to speak of Professor Green as one who has been prominent in the department of Biblical criticism. The spirit of inquiry which marks the present century has not made an exception of the books held sacred by Christendom. New discoveries concerning the institutions, religions, and languages of extinct nations have been made to throw light on Jewish history and Jewish literature. There has also been made a microscopic examination of that literature itself, a comparison of one part with another, and an energetic attempt to determine when, by whom, and for what purpose every part of the Bible was written. Such an investigation was not only inevitable, but desirable. All truth is a good; and the more important the department of study, the more valuable are the results of research in it. And though at present disagreement and indecision may seem to be the only result reached, the ultimate issue cannot but be the furtherance of the cause of truth.

The differences in the methods used and in the conclusions arrived at depend largely, if not mainly, on the differences in the prepossessions with which the various critics enter upon their work. Prepossessions, it is often said, are obstacles in the search after truth, and ought to be laid aside. In fact, however, prepossessions are unavoidable and indispensable in all attempts to enlarge the boundaries of knowledge. Whatever convictions and conclusions a person has gained on any point constitute a body of prepossessions which he must and should carry with him in his further research. He would be a fool if at every step in his progress he should allow himself to unsettle those convictions and attempt to build up again from the very foundations. Indeed, progress in knowledge would in such a case be impossible.

Professor Green, while he believes in the legitimacy and value of the higher criticism, believes, also, that there are right and wrong prepossessions which may be carried into it. While he would adopt the maxim, " Prove all things; hold fast that which is good," he would adopt as a fundamental assumption and criterion the general truthfulness of the Christian Scriptures, as having been established by nineteen centuries of Christian history and Christian apologetics. This fundamental assumption, however, does not prevent him from examining dispassionately all the speculations and alleged discoveries which others have made and which often run counter to the traditional beliefs of Christendom. Rather, it enables him to apply to them a safe and sound test. It qualifies him to act as a higher critic in the highest sense of that term. Furnished as few others have been with a store of such knowledge as pertains to his department, he has been enabled to understand the bearings and the merits of all the manifold theories that have been propounded in regard to the books of the Old Testament. He is familiar with the languages, the history, the archæology, the hermeneutical principles which are concerned in the critical investigations. And with all, and above all, he has a faith in revealed truth and a comprehensive view of its relation to the purposes of God in human history, such as serve to give balance and steadiness to his critical judgments. Some men say that he is prejudiced. Yes, he is prejudiced in favor of the belief that God has revealed His will and purposes to men; in favor of the reality of the redemptive work of God begun in Israel and finished in Jesus Christ; in favor of the credibility of the sacred books which have been handed down as the record of that work and as the oracles of God to guide men to eternal life. And to those who would clamor that such prejudice is treason against the cause of truth he would doubtless say, in the words of Patrick Henry: "If that be treason, make the most of it."

It is with this preconception that Dr. Green approaches the topics of Biblical criticism. His work has been constructive as well as defensive. But the Christian public knows him best on the apologetic side. More than thirty years ago, when Bishop Colenso raked together all the difficulties which he could find in the Pentateuch, Dr. Green came to the defence in his work entitled "The Pentateuch Vindicated from the Aspersions of Bishop Colenso." The task was not a very difficult one; his antagonist, coming forth with all the self-confidence of a Goliath, was easily felled by a few well-aimed stones from the Professor's sling. In that work Dr. Green exposed in a caustic way the weakness of a criticism which magnifies every trifling appearance of difficulty or discrepancy into evidence of ignorance or dishonesty on the part of the Biblical writers—the result being that the marks of ignorance, if not of dishonesty, were found to be on the side of the critic rather than of the books criticised. Since that day little has been heard of the great arithmetical argument against the credibility of the Pentateuch.

During the twenty years that followed Professor Green's masterly reply to Colenso, his contributions to the public consisted chiefly of articles in the periodical press, the most of which had to do with Old Testament subjects. He published also his valuable work on "The Argument of the Book of Job," which, however, is more exegetical than critical, though it incidentally bears upon some critical questions relating to it. It was during this period that Old Testament criticism was taking on a new phase. The dissection of the Pentateuch and the attempts to determine when its several parts were written had hitherto left the main features of Old Testament history unassailed. Certain parts of the Old Testament had been challenged as unauthentic. The Mosaic authorship of the whole Pentateuch had been denied. But it was not generally held that he wrote none of it; and the substantial correctness of the Pentateuchal history was not denied. But now all is changed. Within the last quarter of a century a theory which had been only sporadically propounded before has succeeded the others, and is in its bearings on Christian faith radically different. The Graf-Wellhausen doctrine involves a direct assault on the general authenticity of the Pentateuch and a large part of the other Old Testament books. It requires those who accept it to assume the Pentateuch, with few exceptions, to be a compound of myths, legends, and deliberate fiction. It asks us to regard the Deuteronomic and Levitical legislation as having been concocted centuries after the time of Moses, and to suppose that these productions were fraudulently ascribed to Moses and that the people were somehow deluded into accepting them as really Mosaic. It declares that we cannot be sure that Moses wrote anything. It requires us to hold that Jesus and the New Testament writers were wholly mistaken as to the main facts about the history of the Jewish religion and institutions. It asserts that all Jews and all Christians up to recent years have been radically deceived on these points; and it now asks the world to believe that this long-standing deceit has been unmasked by the mere sagacity of modern critics, although they have discovered no facts material to the case which have not been open to the world through all these centuries.

One may well wonder that such a theory, so revolutionary in its nature, should have succeeded in gaining so much currency as it has among even Christian scholars. The explanation is to be found largely in the very audacity of the hypothesis. Applying the popular principle of evolution, these new critics decided that Judaism could not have begun with a pure monotheism, such as is ascribed in Genesis to Abraham, but must have been developed out of a primitive fetishism and polytheism. Abraham himself was therefore remanded to the region of fable or myth, and even Moses was declared to be a man of whom we know nothing surely. Ethic monotheism was averred to have originated with the prophets who flourished a century and more after the time of Solomon. Things were turned end for end. The historic order, we were told, was really not: The law and the prophets, but: The prophets and the law. Such a "result" of criticism seemed like something "worth the while." It was startling, and therefore attractive.

But such an hypothesis could not expect to be left unchallenged. Against it were arrayed two classes of critics, who, on the question of the critical partition of the Pentateuch, had been on opposite sides. On the one hand, scholars like Professors Strack, of Germany, and James Robertson, of Scotland, leave the question of composite authorship untouched, or even accept the general conclusions of the critical analysis, while yet they sturdily combat these radical conjectures and inferences as to the course of Old Testament history and the general credibility of the Old Testament records. Representing the other and more conservative class of critics, so far as the critical partition is concerned, Dr. Green yet joins hands with such men as these on what must be regarded as the most vital point, viz., opposition to the theory which pronounces the Old Testament as a whole to be largely, or even mainly, unhistorical.

The twenty years following Professor Green's reply to Colenso had not been idle years. And he was now fully prepared to enter into the new conflict which had been begun. The radical criticism, emanating from the new German and Dutch schools, had been made familiar to English readers by Robertson Smith's works, "The Old Testament in the Jewish Church" and "The Prophets of Israel," and by the translation of Kuenen's work on "Prophets and Prophecy in Israel." These books were taken in hand by Professor Green in his "Moses and the Prophets," and subjected to a brilliant critique. The scholars whom he here confronted ranked as coryphaei among the extreme critics of the modern school. It is safe to say that on every point their American opponent showed himself fully their equal in minute acquaintance with the questions at issue, and more than their equal in his ability to take a comprehensive view of the meaning and relations of the Old Testament books and institutions. The result is that he exposes clearly and mercilessly their hasty inferences, unfounded assumptions and manifest blunders, and demonstrates how much less serious the difficulties are on the traditional theory than on the new one.

Particularly effective is his exposition of the fundamental weakness of the critical basis on which the radical hypothesis was founded. In order to establish the new view of the course of Old Testament history, it was necessary to depend on *something* in it as trustworthy. If every part of the Old Testament were fabulous and fictitious, it would be manifestly impossible to enucleate from it any trustworthy historical narrative. Accordingly, the prophetical and certain of the historical books were fixed upon as generally truthful; and by means of them it was sought to show that the Pentateuch, or rather the Hexateuch, was almost entirely untrustworthy. But soon it appeared that these very books, which were selected as the basis of the attempted reconstruction, themselves very largely presuppose or affirm the traditional conception of the order of Old Testament history. And therefore the critics in question found it necessary to run the critical pruning-knife through their own authorities, and eliminate or amend everything which ran counter to their own theory. They had to assume that the final redactors of those books had entertained a false conception of the facts of Jewish history, and that, therefore, even the most trustworthy of the Old Testament books had been largely vitiated by the interpolations and working-over which they had received from these partisan editors. Seeing, then, that the only sources on which they could rely were thus admitted to be unreliable, it seems to savor more of critical audacity than of critical judgment, when, nevertheless, they push on with their conjectures, and profess to be able at every turn, by bare critical insight, to know what to accept and what to reject. As Professor Green admirably observed respecting them, "It would be better to remand the entire history of Israel to the region of fable, and to confess that we have no positive knowledge about it, than to attempt this revolutionary process of reconstruction, which is professedly based upon authorities which are perpetually discredited."

A few years later (1885) Dr. Green published his Newton Lectures on "The Hebrew Feasts," in which he deals with a particular topic much debated in connection with the problem of Mosaic legislation. This treatise is a more elaborate and exhaustive one than that above mentioned. The premises and arguments of the radical critics are carefully considered and conclusively answered; and it is satisfactorily shown that the alleged difficulties found in the different precepts relating to the Jewish festivals do not warrant the hypothesis of a post-Mosaic origin of any of them. This work has had the honor of being translated into German, and Professor Green's writings in general are highly esteemed in Germany by the more conservative Old Testament critics.

Besides rendering these services in defence of the general authenticity of the Old Testament, Dr. Green has devoted much time to the narrower question of the genuineness and integrity of the Pentateuch. Of those who still maintain the essentially Mosaic origin of the Pentateuch it may without hesitation be said that he is the foremost representative. No one else has followed the critical analysis through all its windings so patiently and thoroughly; no one else is more familiar with all the modern works bearing on the subject. He has waged no war against the higher criticism as such. On the contrary, he has freely admitted the legitimacy of critical investigations of the literary structure, authorship, and history of the Biblical books. But he also claims that critical research which tends to the establishment of the unity and Mosaic authorship of the Pentateuch is as truly work in the department of higher criticism as that which leads one to a different conclusion. He can well afford to smile at the egotistic pertness of a man like Professor Cheyne, who can find no genuine and honest criticism except in one who is eager to go to the latest and greatest extreme in the work of upsetting traditional conceptions.

In this field of purely literary criticism it must be confessed that the opposite opinions can, neither of them, be regarded as established by demonstrative arguments. There are features of the Pentateuch which favor the hypothesis of a composite origin; and these indications must be allowed to have their due weight, and cannot be refuted by falling back on the traditional notion that Moses was the author of the whole Pentateuch. But Dr. Green by no means contents himself with this argument. He meets the advocates of the partition theory on their own ground and with their own weapons, and undertakes to prove that the arguments for it are inconclusive. And every one must confess that he has succeeded in showing that, as a strictly scientific and critical question, the unity of the Pentateuch can be maintained by considerations which command respect even where they do not force conviction.

Perhaps the most laborious work of Professor Green has been his examination in the "Hebraica" (1888 ff.) of the current critical partition of the Pentateuch. It required a vast amount of patience and toil on the part of the author; it requires very much, if not so much, patience and toil on the part of a reader to follow the discussion through, and make himself able to appreciate the full force of it. In these articles Dr. Green takes up in the minutest detail the hypothesis adopted by the analysts of the Pentateuch, the philological and other arguments adduced by them, and exposes one by one their inadequacy. Whether or not we are convinced by him of the absolute baselessness of the critical partition, no candid man can refuse to concede that he has exposed a vast number of instances of fallacious reasoning, mistaken assumptions, and hasty inferences. Particularly he shows how, to a very large extent, the hypothesis of diverse authorship determines the critical partition, or, as he felicitously puts it, "The text is partitioned agreeably to a certain hypothesis, every passage having certain characteristics is assigned to one writer, and such as have certain other characteristics to other writers. And when the partition is complete, it corresponds to the hypothesis simply because it was made by the hypothesis." Illustrations of this proposition are given in abundance; and particularly is it shown how the hypothetical redactor is resorted to "for any emergency in the way of transposition, modification, excision, insertion, and readjustment," so that no difficulty in the theory is too great to be overcome by his ever-ready help. Besides all this, Dr. Green shows how the alleged criteria are unwarrantably multiplied by counting in among them words that occur only once, or only in a certain subject, when the use of the words in question really furnishes no evidence whatever of diversity of authorship. The formidable array of linguistic peculiarities of P and J is thus often reduced to a small residuum, showing that, even though there may have been no conscious unfairness on the part of the critics, there has at least been an excessive and inconsiderate zeal to make out a case. And even though this residuum, together with other considerations, may suffice to convince many candid men of the fact of a diversity of authorship, yet Dr. Green's critique of the critical process has at least made it *certain* that no one *can* be *certain* about the correctness of a partition of an ancient work among different authors, when the only data are to be found in the work itself. There may be some strong indications of a plurality of authors, but when one goes so far as to parcel out the work minutely among the several hypothetical writers, undertaking to divide up not only chapters and sections, but verses and parts of verses, to determine what was done by the several original authors and later by revisers and redactors, and to fix the date of these several productions—all this can be regarded as, at the best, only conjecture, which, however plausible it may be made to seem, can from the nature of the case never be proved correct, unless we can discover (what is as good as hopeless) authentic historic information as to the authorship of the books in question. It is one thing to doubt whether Moses wrote all, or nearly all, of the Pentateuch, and quite another thing to find out how many may and who have had part in the work. It is safe to say that human sagacity is not equal to the task; and no amount of agreement among Biblical critics can suffice to warrant any one in pronouncing the partition one of the "results" of scientific research. One may, if he please, hesitate to follow Dr. Green in his positive conclusion that Moses did write nearly the whole work; but no one ought to hesitate to admit that his review of the critical experiments of the last century has demonstrated the essential insecurity of all merely conjectural criticism. And when the furor for novelty in the matter of Biblical theories has passed away, and men are less afraid of believing what their fathers believed, Dr. Green's sturdy and scholarly defences of the traditional faith of Christendom will unquestionably be a powerful factor in destroying the confidence of the Christian Church in the vagaries of a Biblical "science falsely so called," and will help to bring men back from their reckless search for some new thing in religious belief.

Professor Green's contributions to the periodical press on Biblical subjects have been too numerous to mention in detail. But it should be noted that he has not only reviewed many current works on Pentateuchal questions, but has discussed such other mooted topics as the authorship of Isaiah and of Daniel, the titles of the Psalms, and various questions relating to Old Testament prophecy. In all these is seen the hand of a master, in whom conscientious scholarship and humble piety are joined together.

The last year has witnessed the publication of two books by Dr. Green, one of which ("Higher Criticism of the Pentateuch") gives a succinct history of the critical theories and presents the argument on the other side with the clearness and force which characterize all his writings. The other book ("The Unity of the Book of Genesis") gives us the substance of the "Hebraica" articles collected together, and enables the public more easily to follow the controversy concerning the plurality of authorship as related to that book from which the theory of plurality can be most plausibly argued. These two works together furnish a welcome summary of the critical labors of Dr. Green. They are the ripe fruit of long study and profound scholarship. They represent a revulsion from the extreme positions of negative criticism—a revulsion as inevitable and necessary as that which followed the assault made by Baur and his school on the traditional conception of the New Testament. There is a close parallel between the two movements. In both instances a theory of development is the postulate from which the particular deductions are made. In both there is a latent or avowed doubt of the supernatural. In both, an exaggeration of the alleged antithesis of religious tendencies.

In both, the arbitrary ascription of genuineness or authenticity to some books and using them as a means of discrediting others. In both, the distorting of facts for the sake of the theory and the creation of greater difficulties than those that are removed. But in both cases we must recognize the benefit which has come, and is still likely to come, from these attempts to probe to the bottom the time and manner in which the books of the Bible came to be. Though extravagance and even irreverence may characterize some of the speculations, yet the spirit of inquiry which has been awakened cannot fail in the end to lead to a better understanding of the oracles of God. We stand now in a transition period of the conflict. And though for the moment a one-sided and radical hypothesis seems to be the favorite among critical scholars, the lesson of history confirms the intuition of faith, that the ultimate result will be the re-establishment of the credibility and authority of the Word of God in the minds and hearts of men. We may not be able to forecast what the course of the conflict is to be, or what new forms of assault on the foundations of our faith may yet be attempted. But we may be certain of the ultimate result. We will not be greatly moved by the confident assurance with which it is always said of the latest fad of radicalism, that it has "come to stay." We will rather fall back on the assurance of Him who said: "Heaven and earth shall pass away, but my word shall not pass away." And we cannot doubt that high among the higher critics, who by their learning and faith serve to restore and strengthen the faith of others, will always stand the name of William Henry Green.

DR. GREEN'S CONTRIBUTION TO SEMITIC SCHOLARSHIP.

BY THE REV. PROFESSOR J. F. M^cCURDY, PH.D., LL.D.

IT is a great thing to have been a teacher for fifty years. It is a greater thing to have been so long a teacher in Princeton Seminary. It is a great thing to have been a teacher for fifty years. But it is a greater thing to have been for so long a time a teacher of Hebrew. For Hebrew lies at the foundation of things, particularly of the great things with which Princeton is concerned. Princeton has always held that, in matters Biblical and theological, the man who ignores or evades his Hebrew original, though he may do brilliant work, cannot do sound work; he cannot do solid and lasting work. Exegesis is your central study. It is, if you will, the trunk of your tree of knowledge. Its branches are the doctrines of theology and religion. But its roots run deep into the soil of language—the language of the Word of God, the language in which the Old Testament was written, and with which the New Testament is interpenetrated and colored. It is the glory of Princeton that she has always recognized this fundamental axiom, that she has never appealed to the authority either of a Latin vulgate or of an English vulgate.

Instruction in Hebrew was part of the duties of Dr. Archibald Alexander, the first professor in this Seminary. Eight years after the foundation of the institution a special instructor was appointed. The name of that instructor was Charles Hodge, who, two years later, in 1822, was made full Professor of Oriental and Biblical Literature. Four years thereafter Charles Hodge was sent to Europe to study Hebrew, Syriac, and Arabic under the best masters of the time, among them being De Sacy and Gesenius. Again, seven years later, in 1833, Joseph Addison Alexander was appointed instructor in Biblical and Oriental Literature. As instructor and professor in this department he continued to minister till 1846, when William Henry Green was appointed Instructor in Hebrew.

The transfer of functions was completed when, in 1851, Dr. Alexander handed over the chair of Biblical and Oriental Literature to his former assistant.

These appointments mark three distinct eras in the history of Hebrew and Semitic study in Princeton. The first was the epoch introduced by Charles Hodge in 1820. Dr. Archibald Alexander knew only unpointed Hebrew. In fact, he never fully believed in the other more elaborate system. Dr. Hodge's scholarship was of a comprehensive and, so to speak, of a dynamic kind. He cared for and gave out results rather than processes. Minute attention to linguistic forms was never one of his characteristics. Yet his teaching was stimulating and effective. The interest aroused in the original languages of Scripture during his term as instructor must have been great, since we find that, in 1822, the junior class of that year, consisting of twenty-eight members, agreed to raise $7,000 in five years for a professorship in Oriental and Biblical Literature, and the senior class $4,000 for a like purpose. The great merit of Dr. Hodge's work was that through him the study of Hebrew and Greek was made an urgent order of the day for Princeton Seminary.

A great step forward was made with the accession of Joseph Addison Alexander. He was a Hebraist and linguist *con amore*, a philologist in the broadest and deepest sense. His acquisitive power was so great that thoughts and their expression seemed to come to him as undivided wholes by a species of intuition. At least, he appeared to have no consciousness of a *process* in his appropriation of a language or its literature. Hence, in his teaching it was not easy for him to set forth a methodical and normal process of acquisition. He came upon his students with an almost overpowering rush of information. So copious, energetic, and rapid was it that it was apt to carry the ordinary man off his feet, and land him high and dry outside the course, only to be carried forward by side currents or by waves of extra force and reach. Fortunate were those who could swim with such a current. It was a rare chance to be carried swiftly onward upon an ever-widening river of truth, to find the depth and breadth of the stream no element of danger, but a means of getting larger scope and freer play for strong athletic limbs.

Pre-eminent among these sturdy and eager swimmers, or, to drop the metaphor, among the ardent and receptive pupils of the great orientalist and scholar, was the man (I should rather say the boy) who now came to inaugurate the third era in Semitic studies in this Seminary.

What Green stood for in the teaching of oriental languages in Princeton was *method* and *system*. Dr. Alexander made his way through the forest for himself, and that always a sure and straight way, never looking backward except to note the rate of advance. His young assistant learned the way and marked every step, for his own assurance and for the helping of those who might follow. He thus had a prime quality of the great teacher—an intellectual self-consciousness, which holds knowledge in systematic form, and can always certify to itself its own attainment. Thus, with rare sureness and clear-sightedness, he became the Hebrew teacher of his generation in Princeton—not in Princeton merely, but in America; in fact, the most influential Hebrew teacher of his time among English-speaking men.

As all the world knows, this influence was exerted mainly through his grammatical works. What are his characteristics as a grammarian? Mainly these two: a deep sense of the needs of learners and an altogether remarkable faculty of clear and adequate statement. As far as method and principles are concerned, we might say broadly that in these works we have common sense applied to language teaching. That is, he solved the problem of enabling the learner to use most speedily and satisfactorily the original text. The two grammatical systems in vogue at the time when Dr. Green's larger grammar appeared came short of adequate fitness—the one by following too closely the grammars of the classical languages, the other by an over-refinement of exposition. It is enough to say that Green's grammatical system, by its lucidity of arrangement, its aptness and preciseness of definition, its sense of proportion in the treatment of linguistic phenomena, enables the pupil to apply at once his knowledge of forms and inflections to the explanation of his text. He thus finds that what are usually thought to be the

dry roots and stems of a dead language are living and fruitful in
the imperishable forms of the very Word of Life itself. This,
then, is Dr. Green's great service to his generation as a master of
languages. But what he accomplished was not merely the sim-
plifying and popularizing of Hebrew study. His treatment of
the phenomena of the language was, at the same time, broad,
scientific, philosophic.

Nor did he fail to cultivate the other languages of the great
Semitic family of speech. We who, as undergraduates, called
upon him for instruction, knew how ready and apt he was,
though more urgently pressed with work than we at that time
could understand, to introduce us to the mysteries of the Tar-
gums, of Syriac and of Arabic. And when a few of us, more
adventurous still, with some trepidation hazarded the request
that he give us an introduction to Sanskrit, this, too, was not
denied us. Indeed, all that was needed to give him a very high
place in the realm of general and comparative philology was a
little more of the time that was all along being devoted to other
things. Professor Whitney had good reason for saying that he
very much regretted that Dr. Green had been obliged to discon-
tinue the study of Sanskrit.

But what would we have, Mr. President? You know much
better than those of a later date what the demands were upon
the time of a professor of Oriental and Biblical Literature in
those early days. It is almost staggering to think of what
was accomplished by the men of those strenuous times. To get
some notion of it we may take a volume of the *Princeton Review* of those decades, enumerate the articles written by Dr.
Green, and note the variety of their subjects. Then we may
add to them the stated work of the department, the daily lectures delivered till 1859 upon as many subjects as now require
the attention of four or five instructors in the Seminary. We
may throw in besides a reasonable or perhaps an unreasonable
amount of preaching. At last, when in 1859 Dr. Addison Alexander was transferred from the chair of Church History to the
New Testament department, Dr. Green must have felt himself
a free man. He had then only to do the work at present performed by three men. The next year, 1860, just after the death

of Dr. Addison Alexander, Dr. Hodge wrote to a friend with reference to the question of filling the New Testament chair: "Dr. Green cannot touch it. He is fully occupied with the Old Testament, its language, its literature, history, criticism, introduction, and interpretation." One would suppose so. Now, it was just then that he began to write his monumental Hebrew grammar, and on August 22, 1861, he wrote the preface to the finished work.

But I have now little time left to speak of the work of our venerated friend as a living teacher. After all, we can best tell the secret of a man's influence from the methods and character of his routine work. We have seen something of Dr. Green's manifold activity. Let us take a specimen year or two out of the time when he was still without any assistant, and the task of professing and teaching the Semitic languages fell upon him alone. One can speak best of what one knows at first hand; and I shall venture to give some reminiscences of my own experience as a pupil of Dr. Green. The class to which I belong, that of '71, exactly bisects the fifty years which we to-day commemorate. When we came under Dr. Green for the Hebrew of our junior year we felt that we were under a *master*. For myself, I knew at the time that I was passing through an intellectual crisis. First, there came the inevitable weeks of mechanical acquisition. They, however, were not many. I can remember two epochs of the first year's course as distinctly as if we were still in the old Miller room sitting behind the curiously carved old desks. The first real revelation came when we were directed to make a systematic collection of the derivatives from each of the roots which occurred in our reading lessons. The unifying principle of our whole study was then revealed at a single stroke. We could now retain and utilize what we had learned, and build up into a system all that we acquired, *as we acquired it*. The next stage came when we passed in the Chrestomathy from the narrative to the prophetical selections. Here, indeed, a new world was revealed, or rather the old world in a new light, by the application of linguistic facts to exegesis. The Fortieth of Isaiah: "Comfort ye, comfort ye my people, saith your God," was now not simply read; it was *heard*.

The Prophet's own voice seemed to be borne across the centuries, laden with his message, so plaintive, so far-reaching, so divinely full and rich with love and promise. Here was linguistic study ministering not merely to taste and judgment, but to the imagination and the heart. Here was the very glorification of philology. Here was the vindication of the Princetonian tradition of thoroughness and fidelity to the primary authentic forms of the spoken and written Word. After that everything fell naturally into its place. The work of the later years, the use of the Septuagint and other versions, the special exegesis, came as a matter of course. The strong characteristic feature of Dr. Green's linguistic training was this, that with intensest energy and unsurpassed skill he impressed upon students in the formative period of their course the true idea of the highest and worthiest use of Hebrew study.

And yet Dr. Green's achievements in oriental philology are not his greatest work, simply because he regards all such study as a preparatory discipline, as an aid to the understanding of the Scriptures, which it is the business of his life to expound. And so as his work has become more specialized he has become a teacher of Hebrew only in the sense that he employs it in his exegetical lectures. And this is as it should be. Thus is the main purpose of his long academic career best fulfilled. If Philology knows herself and her mission aright, it will be her proudest boast that she is the handmaid of Truth, the truth of mind and spirit, the truth about God and man. With Professor Green, at least, "philology" meant always not the love of words, but the love of the Word—rather, I may say more literally still, the love of the Logos.

This is the explanation of his work, of his method, of his style, of his life. As a writer and teacher of manifold achievements and varied activity, one formula expresses and distinguishes him—an expounder of the Word. And the man himself, in the translucence and purity, in the unity and power of his life, may be summarized in one analogous formula—an exponent of the Word. This is the purpose and the passion of a rarely single-hearted and devoted life. Knowledge and reflection, energy and talents, have here perpetually fed the altar-flame. The fire has burned strong and steady within, and without we see the pure, white light, the *candor* of the love of truth and the truth of love. And so we, his old pupils, looking backward and forward, count him happy in his career and work, in the sum of his years, in the measure of his services, in the motive and outcome of his life. There is no drawback or abatement to a life of consecrated love. For "love never faileth; but whether there be prophecies, they shall fail; whether there be languages, they shall cease; whether there be knowledge, it shall vanish away."

DR. GREEN'S SERVICES TO THE CHURCH AT LARGE.

BY PRESIDENT FRANCIS L. PATTON, D.D., LL.D.

MR. PRESIDENT:

I have not the same right to be heard on this occasion as those who have preceded me, for I can hardly claim to be a Hebrew scholar. And yet I am glad of the opportunity that is afforded me of paying my tribute of affectionate regard to Dr. Green, whom I reverence as I reverence no living man. I am asked to speak of Dr. Green's services to the Church at large, and of course I realize very well that his influence goes far beyond the pale of the Church to which he belongs. But while his fame is world-wide, our particular interest in him to-day takes on a local coloring. I cannot forget that Dr. Green is my fellow-townsman, my colleague in the Seminary, my colleague in the trusteeship of the College, the head of my *alma mater*, my revered teacher, my friend. My enthusiasm and the enthusiasm of all Princeton men very naturally, therefore, focalizes itself about the scene of Dr. Green's lifelong labors. We are celebrating the fiftieth anniversary of Dr. Green's official connection with the Theological Seminary of Princeton. Princeton Seminary is known everywhere as one of the centres of theological opinion. It stands, it is true, for a distinct type of theology, but it stands for a great deal more than the theology which is its own. Oxford is a centre of theology also, and while we do not accept the distinct features of the high Anglican theology, we recognize the great service which the Anglican theologians have rendered in the defence of the Nicene faith. Princeton Seminary has done work outside of the five points of Calvinism. Her voice has been heard in many a controversy, affecting alike all believers in evangelical Christianity. Her voice is yet to be heard, and let me say that when she ceases to speak on the burning questions of evangelical theology her glory will have departed. Dr. Green belongs to a body of scholars and theologians who are now giving, and to a body of scholars and theologians — notably the Alexanders and the Hodges—who have given Princeton the conspicuous place she holds to-day as a great centre of theological opinion.

Princeton Theological Seminary is an ecclesiastical institution. It is under the control of the Presbyterian General Assembly, and does its work within the limitations of a well-defined confessional area. I am far from saying that there is or should be no place for the free handling of theological subjects, but I am very sure that that place is not to be found in an institution the final cause of whose existence is the perpetuation and defence of the Calvinistic system. Dr. Green, then, as it is not necessary for me to say, is a Presbyterian and a Calvinist, and the service he has rendered Christendom has been in connection with and as a minister of the Presbyterian Church. Our Church has no reason to be ashamed of the work she has done in any of the legitimate spheres of church work. She has preached the Gospel at home and abroad. She has been interested in the cause of education, and has assumed her full share of responsibility in regard to philanthropic movements. She has contributed to the advancement of theological learning, and she has defended the faith once for all given to the saints; and Dr. Green, through all of his long career, has been one of her trusted leaders. He has not been seen often in church courts, nor is he fond of debate. His life has been that of a modest, retiring scholar, but he has lived in closest sympathy with the life of the Church he serves. In 1891 the Church honored herself quite as much as she honored him in inviting him to preside over the deliberations of her General Assembly. He was a member, also, of the committee appointed by a previous Assembly in reference to a proposed revision of the Confession of Faith. He represented a conservative view of that question, but he was so patient, so gentle, so tolerant of opposing views, so hospitable to suggestion, and so ready to welcome light, so willing to make concessions, and so strong and convincing in the presentation of his own matured opinions in regard to any pending question, that there was no one who commanded, I think, quite so much as he did the deferential regard of the whole committee, and by none was this more freely accorded than by those who, nevertheless, were compelled to adopt opinions differing from his own.

But Dr. Green has lived in an atmosphere of thought less distinctively denominational than that of some of his colleagues, for some of the chairs in a theological seminary are obviously in closer relation with distinctively denominational ideas than others. The Professor of Church Polity, for instance, is obliged to antagonize prelacy, and the Professor of Dogmatics must defend the Calvinistic positions in opposition to Arminianism; but it is otherwise with the occupant of the chair of Hebrew. There is nothing denominational about the "apocopated future" or the "vav conversive." The Roman Catholic and the Protestant have the same interest in the Prophecy of Isaiah. Presbyterians and Anglicans are alike concerned in regard to the truth of the Pentateuchal narrative. One cannot help thinking that there is something specially catholicizing about the department of Old Testament Criticism. One feels about it as Delitzsch does about apologetics, that it is really an irenic discipline; that this is a sphere where scholarship obliterates sectarianism and that, meeting on the common ground of interest in the truth of the Old Testament narrative, Roman Catholic and Protestant defenders of the faith, can greet each other with a hearty *pax vobiscum*. I do not doubt, therefore, that Dr. Green felt quite at home when he took his seat as a member of the company of Old Testament revisers among his brethren of other denominations. I have no doubt, also, that he entered *con amore* with his co-committeemen upon the work of trying to establish a *modus vivendi* between Presbyterians and Episcopalians, which, if it could not bring us together under one corporate name, might, it was hoped, bring us into closer denominational relations. I refer to these services that Dr. Green has rendered because they ought not to be omitted, and there are other services, I dare say, which might also be mentioned. But none of these enter conspicuously into the estimate which we are making of his life. There are some men who are able to do several things fairly well, and their claim to recognition, if they have any, consists in their versatility. But Dr. Green's greatness consists in the fact that he has brought the resources of a powerful intellect to bear upon a single theme, and that he has given it his untiring and undivided attention through fifty years. That theme is the Old Testament. By narrowing his work he has widened his influence; and in what is the latest product of his pen he has made every one his debtor—be he Jew or Christian, be he Roman Catholic or Protestant—who looks upon the Old Testament as a revelation from God.

Dr. Green's services to the Church at large cannot be separated from his service to the Presbyterian Church, for the simple reason that the best way for any man to serve the Church at large is to do his best to serve the church to which he belongs and within the institutional limits which define his life. Dr. Green has been a patient, laborious professor in the chair of Old Testament Literature in Princeton Theological Seminary, and if we wish to know what service he has rendered the Church at large, we must see what he is as a teacher, a scholar, and a defender of the faith.

Dr. Green has honored the teacher's calling. He has not found in the claims of authorship an excuse for seeking release from the burdens of the class-room, and he has revealed to us a secret which all teachers would do well to profit by, to wit, that the way to keep strong in the chair is to keep busy in the study. Dr. Green's teaching has covered the whole field of Old Testament learning. His students have learned the paradigms of the Hebrew verb out of his grammar. They have studied exegesis under his guidance. He has made them acquainted with the Jewish institutions, and has led them through the mazes of Old Testament criticism to safe and sure positions respecting the authority of the Bible. He has not read the Bible with a shake of the head or a shrug of the shoulders. No one has had his faith in the Bible weakened as a result of Dr. Green's teaching, though this result may easily happen when, on the one hand, a strong man betrays sympathy with the sceptical side of the debate, or, on the other hand, a weak man makes ineffectual efforts to defend the truth. Dr. Green's students have always known that he was a devout believer in the Bible as the Word of God, and that he could cope with any man in defending his belief.

A man may be a great teacher without being a great scholar, but it adds immensely to a man's power in the class-room if his students know that he is a recognized authority in the department with which he deals. There never was any doubt in the minds of Dr. Green's students about his commanding position in the field of Hebrew scholarship, and his work is a good example of what we ought to expect in our theological seminaries. I know that the seminary is a place for the practical training of ministers, but it is also a place for advanced scientific research in theology. The professors should be teachers, but they should be scholars, too, and we should have more of them than we now have. There never was a time when learning was more needed than to-day, and it is nowhere more needed than in the sphere of theology. We have men enough, perhaps, who deal with ideas and manipulate notions. We have dialectic enough and rhetoric enough and to spare. We need men who can speak authoritatively out of the abundance of minute and specialized knowledge. We have no lack of men who can parade second-hand erudition, who can adopt the latest theory advanced in German lecture-rooms and set up early in life as the apostles of new ideas or as adepts in the art of drafting articles of compromise between old faiths and new hypotheses. But we need men like Salmon of Dublin, and Lightfoot of Durham, and Green of Princeton, who can come to the consideration of the burning questions in history and criticism with the authority and independence which are the result of ripe scholarship and minute knowledge of the sources, and can speak in a way that will refute error and stop the mouths of adversaries.

And this leads me to say that Dr. Green has rendered his greatest service to the Church as a defender of the faith. We all understand that there has been an attempt on the part of the higher critics of the Old Testament to dissect the Pentateuch, and show that it is composite in its authorship, and that its contents are or can be distributed among certain unknown authors whom they call J, J_1, P, Q and R. I shall not enter upon the complicated algebra of Pentateuchal analysis. Suffice it to say that, whether on the grounds of literary criticism the contents of the Pentateuch be divided between the Jehovist, the Elohist, and the Redactor, or whether on the basis of the evolution hypothesis the three Mosaic codes be made to cover the whole period from Moses to the exile, the effect of this is materially to change our faith in the Old Testament. And I wish to say that the question about the Pentateuch is not a question regarding the inerrancy of the Bible; it is not a question about the inspiration of the Bible; it is a question about the truth of the Bible. The signal service which Dr. Green has rendered the Church is that in connection with this controversy—in his reply to Colenso in 1863, in his Hebrew Feasts, in his articles in the *Presbyterian Review*, in his articles in *Hebraica*, and now in the two books which have just come from his pen—he has been a defender of the historical trustworthiness of the books of Moses. Now, there are several ways in which this problem may be handled; in which, as a matter of fact, it has been handled.

There were those, I suppose there are still those, who say that the theological seminary is not the place to teach the higher criticism, and that the Old Testament professor should interpret the Bible and not try to defend it. I am free to say that I have no sympathy with this view, and I do not think that Dr. Green has. If men suppose that this is the way to deal with students at the present time, they do not understand students.

There are those who seem to think that, having accepted the doctrine of inspiration, they have only to quote from the Bible a statement that the Pentateuch was written by Moses in order to silence the adversary. This is a very easy sort of apologetic. It needs but little learning in order to employ it, and ordinarily those who do employ it have but little. Dr. Green is too wise a man to do this. He knows that the doctrine of inspiration is itself an induction from the facts of Scripture, and that if the facts of Scripture were to force him to an acceptance of the critic's conclusion regarding the authorship of the Pentateuch, he would be forced, also, to modify his views of inspiration.

Again, there are those who deal with the problem by showing the unfavorable consequences which would follow from the acceptance of the theory of Pentateuchal analysis. They show that it destroys all confidence in the truth of the Old Testament; that being part of a naturalistic philosophy of religion, the elimination of the supernatural from the Old Testament will naturally be followed by the elimination of the supernatural from the New Testament. I confess that this is a very important service to render. Hebrew scholars seem sometimes not to know the logical consequences of their theory, which men without any claim to Hebrew scholarship are quick enough to perceive. Dr. Green sees these consequences, and you will find an admirable account of the *status questionis* in his little book on the higher criticism of the Pentateuch. I wish, indeed, that men who think that the Christian world is fighting over a question of inerrancy would read that little book. It would open their eyes, I think, to the magnitude of this Pentateuchal question.

And yet, again, there are those, I think, who approach the subject in the spirit of a concessive apologetic. They say: conceding all that is asked by the higher criticism, it is, nevertheless, true that the gradual evolution of religious thought has reached its climax in Christianity. There has been a gradual unfolding of a Messianic idea that finds its fulfilment in the advent of Christ. There are exceptional facts of an historic kind, such as the conversion of Paul and the resurrection of Christ, which are sufficient to assure us of our supernatural Christianity. And I think that there is, undoubtedly, great value attaching to this form of apologetic. You will observe, however, that none of these methods meet the objectors, for they either assume that the critics are wrong or they are trying to show what would happen supposing they are right.

But Dr. Green has undertaken to show that from Astruc to Wellhausen there has not been a single theory in support of the composite authorship of the Pentateuch that will stand criticism. He has left to others the task of showing what will happen if the critics are right, and he has devoted himself to the task of showing that the critics are wrong. He has come to the study of this problem in the maturity of his powers; he has brought to bear upon it ripe scholarship, minute and intimate knowledge of the Scriptures, and complete acquaintance with the critical literature. And with marvellous patience, with remorseless logic, with great power of statement, with infinite skill in the management of his material, he has put together an overwhelming refutation of the claims of the theorists. He has shown that it is impossible to separate the Pentateuch into a series of different documents, and that, save for the antisupernatural bias that controls discussion, there is absolutely no reason for doubting its Mosaic authorship. This book on the Unity of the Book of Genesis is Dr. Green's masterpiece. It is a masterpiece, I venture to say, in the realm of scholarly polemic. It takes rank among the classics of apologetic literature, and it gives its author a foremost place among the few great apologists of the world.

DR. GREEN'S REPLY.

FELLOW-ALUMNI, BRETHREN AND FRIENDS:

I have no words to express my gratitude for this very touching exhibition of kindly feeling. I thank you, one and all, most sincerely for honoring this anniversary by your presence. It is very gratifying to see again the faces of those well known in former years, who have since been scattered far and near, and now have come up hither to testify their continued affection for and confidence in the *alma mater*, where we alike received our first lessons in theological lore. And we cordially welcome among us to-day the representatives of sister institutions that are co-workers in the promotion of Christian scholarship, whose friendly greetings we are proud to receive and gladly reciprocate. There is no richer earthly treasure than the approval of the wise and good. One must be insensible, indeed, not to be deeply affected by such a manifestation as is here presented. And the graceful words of generous commendation which have been spoken by those whose esteem I highly value are very warmly appreciated, however the utterances may be colored by the partialities of friendship.

Princeton Seminary stands, as it has always stood, for fidelity to the Word of God and the standards of the Presbyterian Church. At the same time it stands for the highest grade of Biblical and theological learning. It welcomes all the light that can be thrown upon the Scriptures from every quarter, and does not shrink from the application of the most rigorous tests to the question of their origin or the nature of their contents. Convinced by the most abundant evidence that these Scriptures are the infallible word of God, and that their teachings are the utterances of divinely sanctioned truth, this Seminary has always maintained that sound learning will ever go hand in hand with implicit faith in this sacred volume.

It was upon this basis that Princeton Seminary was originally founded. It was with the unanimous purpose of establishing an institution where this cardinal position should be firmly held and faithfully inculcated that the Presbyterian Church resolved to plant here this its oldest Seminary. This was the unwavering faith of those who were most directly instrumental in drafting its plan, in laying its first foundations, in giving shape and direction to it in every respect at the outset of its career. This was the fixed and intelligent conviction of its first professors. That splendid quaternion of teachers, Drs. Archibald Alexander, Samuel Miller, Charles Hodge, and Addison Alexander, were the glory and the crown of this Seminary in former years, gave it its reputation before the Church and the world, and in the protracted period during which they were spared to guide its affairs and to conduct its instruction, stamped their own character upon it, as I trust, indelibly. Under them Princeton theology gained a definite and well understood meaning, which, it is to be hoped, it will never lose; from which may it never swerve. They whose privilege it was, as it was mine, to sit at the feet of those great and honored preceptors, will bear their testimony that reverence for the revealed Word of God was a prominent feature of their instructions, and was constantly illustrated not only by the teachings of the class-room, but by their whole spirit and life. And all the wealth of their learning, all the fruit of their reflections, their studies and their researches were made to contribute to the exposition, the illumination, and the exaltation of the Bible.

I happen to be the only remaining link between the original faculty of the Seminary and its present faculty. I was appointed to my professorship and entered upon its duties while the first professor, Dr. Archibald Alexander, still survived. And I can testify that all the professors appointed since, the great majority of whom were trained in this Seminary, have cordially and earnestly taken the same attitude toward the Scriptures that was so steadfastly held by their predecessors. I can confidently appeal to all the alumni of this institution, from first to last, to bear witness, that but one sentiment on this subject has ever found utterance in its halls. And I believe that the great body of those who have gone forth from it to preach the everlasting Gospel of the grace of God in this and other lands have stood firmly by the instructions which they here received on this fundamental matter, and that they have not weakened the power of that divine message which they were charged to bear to immortal men by entertaining or suggesting doubts as to the genuineness of the books of the Bible, or the truth and authority of its contents, or inculcating such a low view of inspiration as would be no guarantee of the trustworthiness of the sacred record.

It has sometimes been said depreciatingly that Princeton stands almost alone and in opposition to all modern scholarship in its adherence to that doctrine of Holy Scripture, which has been the universal Christian creed from the beginning and is embodied in the standards of every historic Church in every land. They who speak thus honor Princeton overmuch. She is not so solitary as some would seem to imagine. Even in Germany university-bred men among the pastors are lifting their voices against the defection of university professors and boldly challenging their positions. There are numerous indications that the scholars of Great Britain are not all willing to follow in the wake of Drs. Cheyne and Driver. And in this country the faculties of nearly every theological seminary in all the various branches of the Presbyterian Church are a unit in maintaining the trustworthiness, the genuineness, and the infallible inspiration of the books of Holy Scripture. And if any one of them has swung off from this common foundation, it has thereby antagonized the faith of the Church to which it professedly belongs, the faith which the Seminary was itself founded to defend and propagate, the faith which its former most distinguished professors devoutly held and constantly taught. And the theological faculties of other denominations of Christians have their numerous scholars who are in full sympathy with all that has ever been taught in Princeton on this subject. We have nothing to boast of in this respect which has not been the common faith of Christendom from the beginning; and so long as the Spirit of God rules in the hearts of men His revealed Word will be held in high honor amongst them. There need be no fear that the Word of God will not triumph in the end, and, in spite of all contradiction, vindicate its right to all that it claims for itself.

Once more, dear brethren, I thank you for your presence here to-day and for the kind and encouraging words which have been spoken in your name. May the blessing of Him, whose we are and whom we serve, rest in rich measure upon you all.

CONGRATULATORY ADDRESSES

FROM THE PRESBYTERIAN CHURCH IN THE UNITED STATES OF AMERICA.

BY THE REV. ROBERT RUSSELL BOOTH, D.D., LL.D.,
MODERATOR OF THE GENERAL ASSEMBLY.

DR. GREEN: HONORED AND BELOVED BROTHER:

It has been made my privilege to participate in these most interesting scenes, by presenting to you, within the limits of five minutes, the congratulations of the Church of which you have nearly all your life been a member, and which a few years ago unanimously called you to its highest position of honor. I am well assured that throughout our great membership there is a common sentiment of approbation and rejoicing over the long, and useful, and happy career which you are here this day to celebrate. It is, indeed, true that no formal resolution has commissioned the present Moderator to speak thus in behalf of the Presbyterian Church. Had the General Assembly been recently in session, or had it foreseen this occasion, there is little doubt that the common feeling would have found some such expression in terms well suited to the career of one who has so well served the Church by example, and influence, and testimony. But we need have no misgivings as to the reality of such a widespread and cordial interest in this celebration. The great heart of our beloved Church is speaking here to-day by this unparalleled assembly of her sons, who, coming from many States and many lands, attest their love and gratitude to the wise teacher, the faithful friend, and the strong defender of the faith.

We recognize on this occasion the noble service you have rendered during these fifty years as a theological instructor. The students you have trained have gone out from under your influence carefully instructed in the language and literature of the Old Testament and bearing the impress of a character dignified, pure, and ever faithful to truth. Thus you have been living through these years in thousands of hearts who now serve the Church in so many fields at home and abroad.

But I must not fail in this brief congratulation to mention the more important service which you have rendered to the Church, in these later years, in that great controversy concerning the authenticity and truthfulness of the Old Testament Scriptures, which has been one of the phases of the larger conflict between naturalism and supernaturalism in our day. The Church has turned to you with strong confidence and calm assurance in this great crisis. This believing Church of God, which has clearly recognized the essential bearing of this question upon the very existence of our holy religion, has seen in you its standard-bearer in this conflict, and has realized that, as it was in the Arian controversy of the olden time, so in this great debate, you have been to us an "Athanasius against the world."

Those two notable books which are the product of your most mature thought and learning, "The Unity of the Book of Genesis" and "The Higher Criticism of the Pentateuch," afford a solid basis for the ministers and members of this Church to stand upon as they maintain its ancient doctrine concerning the Scriptures of the Old Testament. For if it is impossible for a finished scholar, trained by fifty years of special Hebrew study, to have arrived at a knowledge of elemental truth on such a subject, then we may well conclude that there is no rational conclusion possible on the one side or the other.

And so we are content as a Church to take the verdict on this question from one whose character for firmness, whose purity of life and teaching, and whose thorough knowledge of the ancient Scriptures render his decision adequate and final in any age of time.

This, then, is our conviction, and in this spirit we utter our congratulations for the great work you have accomplished as a defender of the faith.

And so to-day this Church of ours, out of its loving heart, sends forth a greeting to the man who has strengthened her hold upon the Bible and has thus given validity to her immortal hope and to her mission of salvation in the name of Christ.

And perhaps it is not an unwarranted stretch of the imagination, if one is reminded, as he surveys the varied features of this impressive scene to-day, of an historical event in old Hebrew history, in the time of the captivity, when Mordecai, the Jew eminent for services to the Persian State, was led through the streets of the city of Shushan, and it was proclaimed before him, while the people rent the air with approving shouts: "Thus shall it be done to the man whom the king delighteth to honor."

FROM OUR SISTER CHURCHES.

BY THE REV. PROFESSOR WILLIAM M. McPHEETERS, D.D., OF COLUMBIA THEOLOGICAL SEMINARY.

Mr. Chairman:

I esteem it a rare pleasure and privilege to be with you on this auspicious occasion. The place and the event alike conspire to fan the enthusiasm of the Presbyterian heart into a flame. Princeton! What Presbyterian—North, South, East, or West—does not know and revere the name? With many of us it is associated with tender ancestral memories; with all of us it stands for whatever is vigorous in thought, sound in philosophy, wise in counsel, pure in doctrine, lofty in principle, and holy and inspiring in example. Fragrant with the memories consecrated by the ashes of our Alexanders, our Miller, our Hodges—not to mention other great and venerable names—if we were not in principle opposed to sacred places, this would certainly be the Mecca of all American Presbyterians. Though not our Mecca, Princeton is in a true and gracious sense the dear and honored mother of us all.

Hence, standing here to-day, confident that I but voice their common sentiment, I extend to this noble school of the prophets the hearty, unqualified congratulations of all upon this continent who bear the Presbyterian name or profess the Presbyterian faith. I congratulate her that she has accomplished with such distinguished success the difficult task of ever making her present worthy of her illustrious past. I congratulate her on the fact that, great as has been her fertility in the past in raising up worthy and able champions for the truth of God, the event we celebrate is itself the most convincing evidence that that fertility is yet as great as ever. May I speak freely, Mr. Chairman? If so, sincerely desiring to give offence unto none, merely giving expression to what I believe to be the feeling of the great mass of American Presbyterians—preachers and people alike—I congratulate Princeton Seminary that in this evil day, when God's Word is, as many of us believe, being betrayed in the house of its friends, her's has been the privilege, her's the honor, of raising up one who, in the opinion of so competent and impartial a judge as Dr. William Hayes Ward, is "by general consent the leading defender in this country, if not in the world, of the authenticity and integrity of the Mosaic books"—high praise, but none too high.

I congratulate her in view of the fact that this celebration, if it means anything, if it is more than an empty pageant, means that Princeton stands pledged to use every effort to rally the entire American Church to the support not of any denominational shibboleth, but of a position vital to the welfare, if not to the very existence, of our common Christianity. I refer, of course, to the position that the Old Testament as little as the New is a "cunningly devised fable," that the Old Testament as surely as the New is "the Scriptures of truth," the oracles of God. For hide it as men may, even from their own eyes, by smooth and fair words, that, and nothing less than that, is the issue with which the Church stands confronted at this hour. No one has more clearly discerned the true nature of the vital importance of the issue which is now, so unfortunately, being thrust upon the American Church than your own distinguished scholar, whom we all this day delight to honor.

And now, venerable father, on behalf of my own dear Church, and on behalf of multitudes of the ministers and people of the American Church, without distinction of name or creed, I congratulate you that God has spared your life and strength to this happy hour; and that as a partial reward of your consecrated labors He permits you to-day to get a glimpse of the high esteem in which both you yourself and your work are held by multitudes of His people in this and other lands.

I congratulate you that the Great Head and Saviour of the Church has qualified you, inclined you, and enabled you to render a service such as few are capable of rendering, and fewer still privileged to render to the cause of truth.

I congratulate you that the scholarly productions of your gifted pen promise to be not only a permanent monument to your own honor and to that of this Institution, but—what is better—a permanent testimony to the truth of God and, by His blessing, an effective bulwark against one of the strongest currents of error that has ever set in against that truth.

I congratulate you that you have been permitted to ground so many hundreds of faithful ministers in sound principles of interpretation; that you have had no mean part in giving to Princeton Seminary its present prestige.

I congratulate you that you have so borne yourself in all your controversies as not only to have won the admiration and applause of your friends, but—what is far harder—that you have so borne yourself as to have secured the genuine respect even of those who have differed from you most widely; their respect for your extensive and accurate learning, your keenness of insight and force of logic, and last, but not least, for a certain lofty candor and courtesy, which, as they had no need, had also no inclination, to substitute declamation for demonstration or abuse for argument.

In conclusion, it gives me sincere pleasure to bring to you to-day congratulatory messages from a large number of representative men who are entitled to speak for their respective churches, and to assure you that it is the fervent prayer of many hearts that the Glorious Head of the Church may spare you yet many years and enable you yet further to enrich her literature with the ripe fruit of your learning and your wisdom, and that He may crown all of His grace toward you here with glory in the life to come.

FROM OUR SISTER SEMINARIES.

BY THE REV. PROFESSOR WILLIS J. BEECHER, D.D., OF AUBURN THEOLOGICAL SEMINARY.

MY REVEREND AND ESTEEMED FRIEND, DR. GREEN:

The delightful task has been assigned me of offering to you on this occasion the congratulations of "Our Sister Seminaries." No definition of the term "Sister Seminaries" has been handed to me, and I prefer to magnify my office by giving the term as wide a meaning as possible. There are some scores of theological schools in North America, manned by some hundreds of professors, cared for by many hundreds of ministers of religion and interested laymen, and attended by some thousands of students. A few of these schools claim to be the older sisters of Princeton Seminary, but a majority of them, probably, have come into existence since your appointment to the chair you hold. In most of them some doctrines are taught which you and I disapprove. In some cases the disapproval extends to a large proportion of the doctrines that are taught. But, taken as a whole, the theological instructors of this continent are godly men, men of learning, men who are devoted to the promoting of the interests of the kingdom of God on earth, men with whom it is an honor to be classed.

It is presumption in me to undertake to speak for so august a constituency; and yet I doubt not that I correctly represent this constituency when I say that we sincerely congratulate you to-day. We congratulate you that you have caused American scholarship to be recognized and respected throughout the Western, the Eastern, and the Australian continents. We congratulate you that no one has ever doubted the earnestness of your convictions or your courage or ability for maintaining them. We congratulate you that, after half a century of service, your insight into truth seems to remain undimmed and your intellectual force unabated; that your latest important work, published a few months since, shows greater learning and greater mental vigor than any of your previous important publications.

We congratulate you that you have in so high a degree that prized reward of the successful teacher, the warm affection and enthusiastic appreciation of the men into whose faces you have looked in the class-room. We congratulate you on the place you hold in the esteem of your associates and of your innumerable friends from all quarters; that the scene of to-day is not a mere ovation, but a true triumphal march; a triumph worthily accorded in celebration of the victories of half a hundred years.

As men interested in scholarship, and thought, and human successes, we tender you these congratulations. But we do not cease here. We are also interested in spiritual things, in God, in eternity, in the historical revelation of Himself which God has made, in the divine redemption for men, in the present Spirit of God, in the holy written Word. We congratulate you that you have for yourself an assured hope of immortality through the saviour, whom you and I worship, as our Lord and God, and that you have led others into the same blessed hope. We congratulate you on the reality of that truth, so influential in your own career, that the Lord God omnipotent reigneth; and that His purposes will not fail, either through the efforts of His enemies or through the mistakes and weaknesses of His friends. In fine, our highest tribute to you is this: that we believe you are pleased to be congratulated not so much on your having served the Master so well as on your having such a Master to serve.

FROM DR. GREEN'S ALMA MATER.

BY PRESIDENT ETHELBERT D. WARFIELD, LL.D., LAFAYETTE COLLEGE.

LAFAYETTE COLLEGE rejoices to-day with unfeigned joy in the career of her son—the child of her youth. I might with truth declare that she reckons you her most distinguished graduate. But she looks upon you too much with the true mother's eye to count your honors or recount your deeds. She cares more for what you are than for what you have done. Her ambition from the time that the wise Junkin wedded her to eternal truth has been to make men

"Wise, steadfast in the strength of God, and true."

And she has watched with gladness all these years the proof you have given of the early blessing that has rested on her dearest wish.

As you look back, over the nearly sixty years that intervene, to the day when you entered Lafayette College, you look upon a day of small things. It was a very small and unpretentious building that boasted the name of college, the faculty were few and comparatively undistinguished, the students were not many, and very youthful—yourself almost the youngest of them all. But in the teachers and the students there was a purpose deep and strong which has given them and the college a claim upon all this country; in the beautiful situation there was an inspiration sure to find expression in later years; and in God's providence there was a large place for the future of the college and the men who sat beside you in the class-room. You will doubtless recall some of those familiar faces to-day, but a few of whom remain to testify to the vigor and force of character of the able class of 1840. Samuel W. Barber, Dorris, and Porter are of those few; William E. Barber, Chauvenet, Elliott, and Richey are of those who have gone to receive the reward of long and useful lives. They all testify to the same consecration to the service of God.

It has been your peculiar privilege to occupy a position in which you have been able to render a great and notable service to the highest truth. In a day of prevalent apostacy, in a time when knowledge is exalted and wisdom is despised, you have embraced the opportunity, which so many have refused, to speak words of soberness and strength in defence of the Word of God. Your *alma mater*, mindful of all your faithfulness in many labors, congratulates you especially on the courage and modesty which have united to make so great a service possible.

Like Ruth, our college was won to the Church from an alien origin, and, like Ruth, God has made her the mother of many of the faithful. It has been her delight to send these sons to sit at your feet. However great her solicitude has ever been for the future of her children, she has never had one moment's anxiety for what they might learn here. She has known too well how devoted has been your service of the dear Elder Brother of us all to fear that in your teaching anything could intrude which would lead these younger brethren away from the old lessons of faith and duty. God grant that you may long continue to open to successive classes the Word of God, and for yourself,

> May you live
> Longer than I have time to tell the years
> Ever beloved and loving. . . .
> And when old time shall lead you to the end
> May you and goodness fill one monument.

FROM THE TRUSTEES OF PRINCETON COLLEGE.

BY HENRY M. ALEXANDER, LL.D.

I FEEL honored that I have been selected by the Trustees of Princeton University to convey their congratulations to your eminent guest. When Dr. Warfield notified me of the desire that I should represent the College upon this occasion, he kindly referred to the hereditary claims that the Seminary had upon me. He might have added that there were hereditary personal reasons why I should be called upon to present congratulations to one of the Greens. I recall the fact that the most intimate friends of my father and mother were the grandfather and grandmother of the eminent man in whose honor we are assembled to-day. I well remember the frequent visits of my parents to his grandparents more than sixty years ago. As a little boy, I was taken to Lawrenceville on those fortnightly visits, and I shall never forget the interesting and animated conversations to which it was my privilege to listen. I recall, also, the expressions of my parents, on the way home, of admiration of their hosts, and particularly for the talents and cultivation of their hostess, Mrs. Green, whose memory has been preserved with filial gratitude by her descendants.

It is a notable family; and they are mistaken who suppose that the princely gifts to Princeton of one of this family is the chief cause of the honor in which the name of Green will always be held at Princeton. I can speak freely of those great and good men—now no more—who have been distinguished judges in this State; and I might speak, also, of those of the family still members of the Board which I represent, who are ornaments of the bench and bar of New Jersey.

It is scarcely necessary for me to express the sentiments of the Trustees of the University upon this happy occasion. I could not do so as effectually as they themselves have already done in a time that is past. For, upon the retirement of Dr. Maclean from the Presidency of the College, they unanimously elected Dr. William Henry Green to be his successor. The Seminary rejoices that he felt constrained to decline the offer of this high position.

Permit me, Dr. Green, to express to you the admiration of the Trustees of the University of your great learning and ability, which have added lustre to the Seminary associated with the names of Miller and the Hodges. They instruct me to express their wishes and prayers that you may long be spared to continue to be the pride and glory of the venerable Institution in which we all feel so great an interest.

FROM THE OLD TESTAMENT REVISION COMMITTEE.

BY THE REV. PROFESSOR HOWARD OSGOOD, D.D., LL.D., OF ROCHESTER THEOLOGICAL SEMINARY.

DR. GREEN was always the Chairman of the Old Testament Revision Committee. It was composed of professors drawn from six different churches; men of positive views in theology and scholarship, differing widely on minor points. From all those thirteen years of mutual prayer and common aim there remain memories that are sacred. They were years of unceasing activity, of clashing argument, of remorseless voting. Each member in turn, including our revered Chairman, at times found himself alone in his view. But never from any of these meetings did a member bear away the sting of a single discourteous word or suggestion.

Across the wide fields of scholarship, over the paths of unlimited freedom of debate, around difficulties that threatened to become positive obstructions, our Chairman led the company safely to the end of its task.

Every member would gratefully ascribe a large part of that record to the wise, patient, gentle example and rule of our Chairman. We look back with gratitude to the years spent with Dr. Green, and we rejoice with you in this celebration of his fifty years of noble service.

AFTER-DINNER SPEECHES

THE "FATHER OF THE MAN."

BY THE REV. WILLIAM C. CATTELL, D.D., LL.D.

IF there be truth in the familiar line of Wordsworth, "The child is father of the man," our reminiscences to-day should certainly include that child who was father of such a man as Dr. William Henry Green, and I imagine that the Committee of Arrangements assigned this subject to me in particular because as the senior member of the Seminary Board of Directors it was presumed that, among all my colleagues, my memory would reach farthest back beyond that half-century of his life which we are here met to celebrate. This may be so; and it is certainly true that, as the programme has it, I was "Sometime President of Lafayette College," upon whose roll the name of William Henry Green was written while he might still be called a child—for he was barely twelve years old when he was matriculated. It would not be inappropriate, then, to expect from me something with regard to him as a "college student." For, although I was not connected with Lafayette until long after he was graduated, two of his classmates were my colleagues in its Board of Trustees and with two others of his class I had still more intimate associations as colleagues in the faculty. From them and others of his fellow-students, and from his teachers also, I have learned at first hand not a little about his college days—much more, indeed, than I can tell in the few minutes allotted to my speech.

I will begin with one thing that may surprise you. Dr. Vanderveer, an old-time teacher of great ability, and for some years principal of the preparatory department of the college, told me that William Henry insistently and earnestly begged to be excused from the study of the languages on the ground that he had no aptitude whatever for them. Fortunately, the lad listened to the advice of his revered instructor, and went on in the study of his Latin and Greek, developing into the marvellous scholar in languages whom the world honors. This incident is worth passing along in this age, when optional or elective courses of study are so abundantly provided for college youth on the supposition that they best know what their own aptitudes are.

You will anticipate me when I say that from the beginning of his college course he was regarded as the best scholar in his class. He graduated with its highest honors before he had reached his sixteenth year. One of his classmates, Colonel William Dorris, who has himself made a distinguished career, says: "In pure intellect I place him above any student I ever met. He was perfect in mathematics and in languages, outranking us all in a pretty strong class." My honored friend has certainly put himself under some restraint in speaking so modestly of his class. It was more than "a pretty strong" one. Although small, it was really a remarkable class. Of the eleven members who won their first degree nearly all became eminent in Church or State. Emerson has said: You send your son to the schoolmaster, but it is the boys in the school who teach him. It can be well understood what a factor in the development of our friend was his daily and intimate contact with classmates of such brilliant promise, all of them older than himself.

But there were eminent teachers in the faculty. Among them, and *facile princeps*, was that marvellous man, Dr. George Junkin, who exerted such a powerful influence on the whole college community. The range of studies at Lafayette in those early days, as well as the small number of students, made the contact between professor and student close and frequent. I need not remind you that the true teacher is greater than his book, and his personality a most important element in culture.

The young collegian was remarkable for more than "pure intellect." The traditions of the elders all represent him as leading a blameless and winsome life among his fellows, always prompt and conscientious in the discharge of every duty. So much did I hear of his exemplary deportment that I often, in a bewildered sort of way, tried to imagine what a life I should be leading as the college president, had all the students been like William Henry Green!

I must emphasize one thing about his fidelity. He was not only prompt at every recitation, but he never missed college prayers in the chapel at five o'clock in the morning, winter and summer! Dr. Junkin, a Covenanter Presbyterian of the old Scotch type, was brought up on the Psalms. He could sing with David, "I myself will awake right early," and he did not fail to wake the college boys right early that they might sing with him.

But William Henry, notwithstanding his perfect recitations in the class-room, does not seem to have been a laborious student. In fact, his classmate, from whom I have already quoted, says: "We used to play chess together; he was fond of the game, and was a skilful player. But I don't remember ever having seen him study; he seemed to take in every task as if by intuition." Another of his classmates, Dr. Porter, now and for many years past a professor at Lafayette, eminent among the scientists of the age, has told me that he and William Henry read together, in the French translation, the whole of Tasso's "Jerusalem Delivered." This is a further evidence that his time was not wholly taken up with preparations for the class-room, and also that his taste and aptitude for the study of language had already developed. And there is a tradition at Easton—in fact, I heard it again recently from the registrar of the college — that our young friend during his undergraduate course read through the entire Hebrew Bible. This, however, is one of the traditions that cannot be substantiated. But one cannot help wishing it were really true, and falls to wondering what would have been the harvest of Semitic literature in the fifty years that followed had these Hebrew roots been indeed planted so early in such congenial soil.

Most of us know Dr. Green only as the learned scholar, the revered instructor, the preacher whose sermons have been to us like a solemn message from one of the old prophets. This very morning, when his venerable form came into view, as he descended the steps of this platform to take his seat in the presence of the vast audience, how natural it was for us all to rise to our feet, by one spontaneous impulse, and stand before him in profound reverence! It is hard for us to think of him as a college boy, such as he is recalled by the surviving members of his class. One of them, looking back to those early days, nearly sixty years ago, sends me this pleasing picture of him as he was then: "He was a sunny-faced, bright-eyed boy, quiet, diffident and unassuming in manner, always in a good humor." We can readily believe this; and can well understand that, while his intellectual endowments and his pre-eminent scholarship commanded the respect of his fellow-students, his unassuming manner, his sunny face, his gentleness, and unfailing good humor won their love.

But with these few words we must take leave of the child, who was "Father of the Man," whose personality, through half a century of distinguished usefulness and honor, is to be presented to us by the speakers who are now to follow. We take leave of him in that old-time borough of Easton, with its quiet, peaceful, Christian homes of half a century ago, and in the blessed environment of a college founded by Christian men and for Christian culture. There, all unconsciously to himself, God was preparing him for the illustrious career which was to follow; and there, after the pattern set by the Divine Teacher, to whose service the whole life of our friend has been consecrated —be it said reverently—"The child grew and waxed strong in spirit; filled with wisdom; and the grace of God was upon him."

OUR FELLOW-STUDENT.

BY THE REV. THEODORE L. CUYLER, D.D.

THE brother who prepared this programme for the afternoon is open to a bit of "higher criticism." I am set down here as the "fellow-student" of the honored hero of the day. I was more than that, I was his classmate, and closer, even, than that, for my seat was next to him in the farthest corner of the dear old oratory. And I only regret that my fellow-classmate is not here now that I might look in his eyes and say something to him out of the fulness of my heart; so I shall make him constructively present.

This is the jubilee-day of all the surviving members of the Class of 1846. To our class belongs the honor of giving two professors to Princeton Theological Seminary. Both names are household words through all our Presbyterian realm. One of them was Archibald Alexander Hodge; the other was William Henry Green.

"Archie" Hodge, as he was known among his fellow students, came into our class at the start—young, shy, unpretending, and not conspicuous; in fact, we had a sort of compassion on him as likely to be smothered under the combination of his two great names. What would become of a man who was Archibald Alexander and Hodge rolled into one? He did not display, until he went out to his field of labor at Fredericksburg and Wilkes Barre, his unique and truly splendid gifts. Then we discovered that the name was well given to him and was a prophecy.

William Henry Green came into our class at the beginning of the third year, from Lafayette College, where he had been and where he had struggled after higher mathematics. Tall, very modest, manly, twenty years old by the almanac, he had attained a most remarkable maturity. He leaped at once to the front, the foremost scholar of the class, the foremost scholar in the Seminary. He took to Greek as if he had been born at Athens; he took to Hebrew as if he had been the son of a rabbi in Jerusalem. He seemed to us not so much as a student, but as an incipient professor; and so it was the most natural thing in the world that he stepped at once from the bench of the pupil to the chair of the instructor.

With what immense industry, and consecrated devotion, and superb wealth of scholarship he has adorned that chair for fifty years the whole Christian world knows full well—aye, and some of the foes of sound Biblical scholarship know it to their sorrow. Our class to-day, the few that are surviving, are ready to reach up the greenest laurel we could gather to crown his honored head, and say to him: "Many of our class have done virtuously, but thou hast excelled us all."

One secret of the power and perennial influence of Professor Hodge and Professor Green is that they were always true to the Princeton idea. Now, the Princeton idea in theology is not to invent, but to discover; to be always discovering what Almighty God has revealed to His people, and then to send out an army of young men to proclaim that divine revelation.

This idea was happily illustrated by Archibald Hodge when he was once a guest at my table in company with a graduate of Yale Theological Seminary. The Yale man was inclined to make game of Princeton as rather fossilized. Brother "Archie," in his quaint, characteristic way, said to him, "The trouble with you Yale theological professors is that you only teach your student to think. Thinking sent Adam out of Paradise. In Princeton we let God do the thinking, and teach the students to believe." And it is just because the dear old Seminary has always maintained that listening, reverent attitude toward Jehovah that it has maintained its commanding influence in the land and throughout all the world as the great, impregnable stronghold of sound Biblical theology. One of the controverted questions of the day is, has the Church of God got any Bible? Princeton thunders back, "She has!" "*She has!*" And we stand by it from the Genesis clear through to the last hallelujah of the Apocalypse.

The great thing about William Henry Green—the grandest thing about him, is not his intellectual acumen or his massive erudition; it is the beautiful combination of docility and courage that has distinguished all his career. He has sat at the feet of the Infinite Wisdom with the teachable spirit of a little child; he has risen up from that position to contend with the splendid prowess of a Paladin.

To-day a few of his surviving classmates of 1846, the few of them that are left—our heads whitening with the frosts that never melt—gather to join in his coronation. Reminiscences are too sacred to me for jest. I have none to give you. To-day he, with two or three of us, looks back through the vista of fifty years to the days of "Auld Lang Syne." The veil lifts; we are again in the dear old oratory, plain and Presbyterian in its aspect, with the countenance of John Calvin looking down on us from the walls. Archibald Alexander, clad in his old blue cloak, enters and mounts the rostrum. Beside him is the venerable white head of Samuel Miller, and on the other side are the ruddy cheeks and Napoleon-like head of that marvel of many-sided genius, Joseph Addison Alexander. Charles Hodge comes in, limping and leaning on his cane.

We look back to-day and gaze at that wonderful—most wonderful—group through eyes welling out with tears ; and here we see, at the end of half a century, thanks be to God, that the teachings of these glorious men are still taught here ; that the methods pursued here fifty years ago are pursued here still ; and that the tides of innovation and revolution, that have swept away many men and institutions, have swept by and left unharmed the immovable adamant of Princeton Seminary. Stand fast, stand fast, Crag Ellachie!

William Henry Green, illustrious and beloved classmate, to you, more than to any other living man, Princeton has entrusted her standard of purity, truth, and unwavering loyalty to the sacred Word. Right gallantly hast thou borne it aloft in many a hard conflict.

At the close of the day of Agincourt, King Henry rode over the field and came upon a standard-bearer bleeding to death, the standard still grasped in his hand. The king knighted him on the spot. And when the last hour comes for our beloved friend—and distant, far distant, be the hour when it shall come —he will be found lying on the battlefield for Christ, holding the snow-white standard of Princeton in his hand; and the King of Kings will crown him with glory and honor.

THE YOUNG PROFESSOR.

BY THE REV. A. A. E. TAYLOR, D.D., LL.D.

THE students of Professor Green are scattered throughout the known world. Probably the great majority of them in this land are distributed to the West.

It was a critical period in the history of the Seminary, then nearing its fortieth year, when, at the age of twenty-six, Mr. William Henry Green assumed his professorship. The first group of great teachers was rapidly passing. In the previous year the stately and elegant Dr. Samuel Miller had fallen asleep, and his chair remained unfilled. The classical and courteous James W. Alexander had returned to his New York pastorate, his place being still vacant. The venerable Archibald Alexander finished his course a few weeks after the young professor took up his task. Only two professors were left standing beside him. They were Charles Hodge, just mounting to the meridian of his strength in Greek Exegesis and Didactic Theology, and Addison Alexander, resigning to the new professor Biblical and Oriental Literature, to enter upon his brilliant and diversified course in Biblical and Ecclesiastical History. To succeed Addison Alexander, to parallel the Greek exegesis of Charles Hodge with his Hebrew work, and to stand alone with these two experienced co-professors, for the time at least, was the difficult position assigned to him. The Seminary was feeling the shock of its broken faculty. The number of entrants for the new year was 42 as against 65 for the previous year and 55 of the year before that. Also the funds were at a discouraging ebb. There were likewise some difficult students for a young teacher to tackle, such as Robert Watts, James P. Boyce, of South Carolina, Caspar Wistar Hodge, and Isadore Hoewenthal, the learned Jewish convert and Hebraist.

Besides, the fame of the Princeton professorial pulpit for spiritual unction and eloquence was at its height, and must be maintained on a level with the grade of Drs. Miller, the three

Alexanders, Charles Hodge, and the famous College presidents. These men and their compeers were also reaching a high mark of scholarship and literary culture in the *Princeton Review*. Well may the junior professor have trembled in his shoes at the prospect. Yet, however much he may have shrunk from the weighty responsibilities confronting him, he did his trembling in private. To all outward appearance William Henry Green was as self-poised a professor as he is to-day the first time he sat down behind his desk in the class-room, or the hour he took his place beside his spectacled colleagues in the oratory at the Sabbath afternoon conference. Dignified, self-possessed, firm, with a modest embarrassment of manner held under control by the courage of a conscious call of duty, and a certain confidence of one who knows that he is loaded for action, he assumed his position as though he were to the manner born.

Your speaker was a sprightly sophomore of seventeen in the College when Mr. Green returned to Princeton as professor. Being thrown closely by association in the social circles of the younger members of the families of the two faculties, he had heard much of the exalted pulpit reputation of the young professor, who had supplied the newly organized Second Church during a part of the time while he had served as instructor. When young Charlie Hodge first pointed him out on the Seminary grounds he was not playing hand-ball or football. He was making a bee-line, with rapid strides, from his lecture-room to his study. That bee-line is one characteristic secret of Professor Green's pre-eminent scholarship and present position. That tall, solemn, somewhat angular form, marked in every movement by intensity of purpose and directness of action, was never seen to loiter or dally, and was not anxious for wayside interview or the let-down of companion gossip *en route*. "I must be about my Father's business" seemed to fill the environing atmosphere.

Three years later your speaker entered the Seminary and came under the direct personal influence of Professor Green. There are three points of view from which we may observe the young professor in a general way, being restricted by what is due to his presence here. They are the professor in the chair, outside the class-room, and in the pulpit. As a grammatical trainer Professor Green was already working up that condensed and orderly systemization that simplified the study and clarified the vision of paradigms and roots, in preparation for his own excellent grammatical works; and his classes received the benefit of his labors. The course in hermaneutics and correlative branches was not a popular one with most of the students, who were eagerly looking forward to practical field-work. But the lectures of Professor Green were always deeply instructive and attractive. So far as he dwelt on "Introduction" his aim seemed to be not so much criticism, or apologetics, as to initiate the student into a living, working knowledge of the Word of God. His presentation of differing opinions seemed fair and unprejudiced, as though calmly estimated from the highest standpoints of sober historical criticism. While, to quote the familiar phrasing of good Dr. McGill, he did not set us to "toil on the treadmill of a barren dialectic," yet neither did he overwhelm us with technical learning beyond our apprehension. Professor Green was not afflicted with the popular Germanic "mania for hypothesis." By some critics he may have been supposed to have lacked a strictly historical and scientific speculative imagination, that out of the head of an Assyrian bull could construct a whole Pantheon of Assyriology, or that could detect a score of authors in the Pentateuch documents.

But he possessed the logical, constructive faculty that could build solidly where it could find adequate building material and firm ground to build upon. His conservatism has proved Professor Green's strength and the basis of unsurpassed public confidence. Dr. Addison Alexander had long been the admiration of the Seminary classes as the prodigious scholar and the prince of teachers. Direct as a shot, clean-cut, incisive, clear as a bell, he was impatient with ignorance and utterly intolerant of stupidity. He despised an idler or a dolt, and sometimes was justly severe and exacting to the recreant, though ever patient and helpful to those who proved in earnest. Between him and the mild, helpful, and suggestive Hodge Professor Green drew a middle line as a teacher. And the students thought that in his somewhat stern, pointed, and searching way he proved as stimulating to study and pressed as much work out of his classes as did his older colleagues. Many of the students were overawed by the calm dignity of good Dr. Hodge and were positively afraid of Addison Alexander, to whom they seemed to impart their own timidity and nervous embarrassment in their approaches. But the youth and friendly reception of the young professor, despite a certain reticent and reserved manner, drew the students in nearer confidence after they had once become acquainted with him.

Out of the class-room Professor Green was friendly and companionable, though forbidding familiarity and not overly given to small talk or discussion of the commonplace. His sense of humor was perhaps somewhat repressed and discovered itself through a sometime sombre covering in a quiet, lurking smile of appreciation. He did not keep bound volumes of the London *Punch* in his library, for his refreshment, as did Addison Alexander. One incident may illustrate: At the reception given by Professor Green to our class upon graduation, Henry Carrington Alexander and myself were standing near, when a classmate approached whose capacity for enjoying a joke was superior to his ability of framing one. He jocosely remarked to Dr. Green, as he saluted, that the professor seemed to be "quiescing in Hholem." "What did you remark, sir?" "I merely observed, professor, that you were 'quiescing in Hholem.'" "Excuse me, I do not understand you," replied the mystified professor. Then followed a labored explanation of vav and quiescents in Hholem, with the figurative sense and practical application, ending with the statement that he only meant that the professor was standing absorbed in silence. The quiet remark that followed, accompanied by a twinkle of the eye, "Yes, sir, I understand now; it's a pleasant evening," proved the utter discomfiture of the adventurous humorist, and was more than the observers could endure, who were soon rolling, convulsed with laughter, on the lawn outside. The rash temerity of addressing Dr. Green with a Hebrew grammatical joke was too absurdly ludicrous to endure. And yet no kinder or more tender spirit, nor one more helpful or ready to relieve a student in his perplexities, ever sat in a professor's study. The watchful interest with which his students have ever been followed by him in their ministry gives proof of this statement.

Absolutely no time is left to speak of the original and instructive content and fascinating, progressive style of the pulpit efforts of Professor Green, whose later preaching is but the ripening and out-bloom of the stately dignity, the rapid utterance, the intense sincerity of mood and manner, and the exhaustive study of his earlier ministrations. It is estimated that not less than 3,000 students have sat at Dr. Green's feet. His students who enjoyed the dew of his youth rejoice to-day to rise up with their successors, even of these latest years, to invoke upon their beloved professor the supreme blessing of the great Teacher of us all.

THE ESTABLISHED TEACHER.

BY THE REV. EDWARD R. GRIFFIN, D.D., LL.D.

THE faculty of theology in a well-known institution are said to have abandoned, a few years since, the Latin thesis as a condition of graduation because of the extraordinary vagaries, both of Latinity and of doctrine, to which it gave occasion. One promising candidate, for example, maintained two propositions: First, there is a moral government of the world; second, there is a way of escape from it. I have not been so long absent from Princeton as to be in danger of any aberration so startling as this, yet I am glad to be assigned to a simpler duty than that so well performed by the speakers of the morning. It is a most welcome pleasure to be permitted to say a few words, not of historical review or of critical estimate, but of immediate personal feeling, and to know that I speak not merely for myself, but as the representative of all the men of my time. I cannot affirm too earnestly in behalf of the classes with which I am most familiar—those of the decade from 1860 to 1870—our concurrence in every word of honor, gratitude, and affection that has been spoken to-day. Many of us count it one of the chief privileges and blessings of our lives that we have been pupils of Dr. Green; our hearts acknowledge an obligation the extent of which we cannot estimate.

Every student of the Seminary during those years will testify to the commanding influence exerted by the Professor of Oriental and Old Testament Literature. I have often recalled, as an admirable example of power on the part of a teacher, the spirit which prevailed in his class-room. The subjects which he taught naturally made greater demands upon time and labor than were made by most other subjects, yet it was not the demands of the subject, but the characteristics of the man, which accounted for the high standard of fidelity to which nearly every one adhered. I well remember the assiduous conscientiousness with which the daily tasks were performed. Some of the students had never been before under so exacting a discipline; for my own part, I know that—little as Dr. Green can have suspected it—I never worked so hard for any teacher. The recollection of what he accomplished through the simple weight and insistence of his personality has always been instructive to me. I do not remember that he ever addressed a word to us in the way of exhortation or of reproof, but the dullest, most unimpressible person could not withstand the contagion of his example, the strenuous earnestness of his nature. It is a great mistake to suppose that a teacher wins the permanent regard of his pupils by indulgent and easy-going methods, by expecting little of them, by being over-solicitous to smooth away all difficulties. We yield our gratitude and admiration to those who have incited us to arduous tasks, which tax our powers, discover to us our resources, and inspire us with new motives and aspirations.

In the life of Charles Hodge there is an anecdote—which may be too familiar for citation here—of one of the early instructors in Princeton College, who was accustomed to say to his pupils: "Gentlemen, you will find the best preparation for death to be a really thorough knowledge of Greek grammar." This sense of the ethical and spiritual value of earnest intellectual work, and especially an intense sense of the obligation incumbent upon a student of theology to pursue his studies in a religious spirit, and as a means of religious growth, was so characteristic of Dr. Green that it expressed itself in his whole bearing. His high and serious temper rebuked indolence, frivolity, and unconscientiousness, and made it impossible for the most careless of his pupils to forget the great purposes which they ought to hold supreme. He was able to bring us to look upon the routine of work as a means of grace and a test of character, and this rendered his instruction not merely reverential, but spiritually edifying and quickening.

One trait in Dr. Green, which we all recognized, was his sense of justice, his fairness, candor, and sincerity. As the part which he has taken in the controversies of the last thirty-five years has been described to-day, I have recalled with satisfaction the fact that he impressed us in this way. If any man needs to be transparently honest, to be above the suspicion of evasion or concealment, to be incapable of taking an unfair advantage, it is he who engages in the discussion of questions which affect the most cherished beliefs and the most sacred experiences of mankind. It is most unseemly and discreditable to import into such high debate anything of artifice or subterfuge, any tricks of rhetoric or of dialectic. Every pupil of Dr. Green knows that the moral qualifications which ought to be found in a theological disputant are his in an eminent degree, that it would be impossible for him to say anything that he does not believe, or to conceal anything that he does believe, or to use any argument of the soundness of which he is not convinced. We well know that in all that he has said and written he has sought only truth. The cause which he has maintained has had in him a champion without fear and without reproach. Of him it may be said : " His means are fair and spotless as his ends."

An occasion like this is highly suggestive and strongly admonitory to those who are concerned in the administration of institutions of education. Mr. Rashdall, in his learned study of the universities of Europe in the Middle Ages, lately published, gives an interesting account of the way in which the earliest of these foundations arose, without premeditation or authorization, as it were by accident, under the influence of attractive and distinguished teachers, and describes how, in due time, the period of organization set in, of charters and statutes, and faculties and curricula, the personal period being succeeded by the institutional. We are witnessing in our day a somewhat similar transition. Our colleges and schools of professional learning may be said to have been, until within a comparatively recent time, in the personal stage; their equipment was meagre and their efficiency was obviously dependent upon the qualities of individuals. The immense material expansion of the past few years, bringing with it an enormous augmentation of the institutional element, involves the danger that we may come to put undue stress upon what is external and instrumental—costly buildings, extensive libraries, imposing lists of instructors—forgetting that an educational institution is great only in the learning, the genius, the personal force of the men who constitute its teaching body. Princeton Seminary has been fortunate in having had among its teachers men of rare and special gifts, who have transmitted their influence through successive generations of students, and have thus created a *genius loci*, which, in the words of Cardinal Newman, "haunts the home where it has been born, and imbues and forms, more or less and one by one, every individual who is successively brought under its shadow." It is this "self-perpetuating tradition" which constitutes the distinctive character, the true reality and identity of an institution of learning. Why is it that men come back here after an interval of years and feel themselves at home, old associations remaining undisturbed in spite of the changes of time? It is because of the survival in the life of the present of influences derived from the master spirits of the past. The chief concern of those who control the affairs of our universities and colleges and professional schools ought to be to see to it that men are secured for the leading chairs of instruction, who are not only competent in point of knowledge, but are capable of impressing themselves in effective, distinctive, and vital ways upon the minds and characters of those under their care. The memorable and delightful scene which we have witnessed to-day—this unanimous and spontaneous outpouring of loyal and grateful respect and affection—shows what can be accomplished by a great and good man working, during a long series of years, in a professor's chair. The lesson deserves to be deeply pondered.

In the name of my contemporaries in the Seminary, I extend to our honored and beloved master most hearty congratulations and assurances of our loving remembrance. May the succession of men such as he never fail in this place.

THE LEARNED DOCTOR.

BY THE REV. JOHN FOX, D.D.

THE form of this theme suggests some inferences, which it may be unwise to press. "The Learned Doctor,"—are there any doctors who are unlearned? In the Pantheon of heathen divinities there be gods many and lords many, according to St. Paul, ranks and degrees of eminence. So in the Pantheon of Christian doctors of divinity, there are reverends and right reverends, D.D.'s, LL.D.'s, and Litt. D.'s—granting that none are, as Rosalind says in "As You Like It," "lacking the burden of lean and wasteful learning." Still there are differences, one star differing from another star in glory; and in the blaze of such a luminary as fills the firmament of learning to-day many of us would be glad to hide our diminished heads in his brightness or borrow some of his glory to shine in.

I have been chosen to speak to-day to represent in some measure the classes who graduated here twenty years ago, and I think that Dr. Cuyler in his turn must submit to a little higher criticism of his speech. He is justly proud of the fact that the Class of 1846 gave the Seminary two great professors, but he is mistaken in supposing that no other class has done so. The Class of 1876 has added two others, of whom we are in nowise ashamed, Benjamin B. Warfield and George T. Purves, worthy pupils of our worthy grand master, whose *Lobgesang* we all rejoice to sing to-day.

The sharpest and most abiding impression made by Dr. Green upon the average student entering Princeton Seminary twenty or more years ago was that he was the very incarnation and embodiment of sacred learning—using those words in their fullest and richest sense. Other learning we had known, coming up from the feet of other masters in academic institutions. He taught us to feel anew the sacredness of all true learning: and he ushered us into a new realm, which seemed sacred in itself and the more because some of the sanctity of his own character was imparted to it. It is hard, indeed, to distinguish now just what our first impressions were as we look back at them from twenty years and more. They are blended with later knowledge—and especially with the multitudinous impressions of to-day. These seem, however, only to bring out more distinctly the first feelings, and it is pleasant now to know that what we felt in impressionable youth may be cherished still as the more discriminating judgments of later manhood. Standing to-day in the very thick of the conflict, face to face with men in the thronging rush of modern life, trying to stem the torrent of doubt and unbelief, it is something to be able to know that we were taught by such a master, and to feel as those felt who could say, "I have sat at the feet of Gamaliel." It is satisfactory to hear not only this chorus of praise to-day from his friends but to know that even in the camp of the Philistines his prowess and pre-eminent scholarship are recognized. Speaking some time ago with a man known for his pronounced antagonism to all supernatural religion, but of high repute as a man of letters, thoroughly appreciative of the Bible as literature, though not as dogma, I referred to a scholar widely known as an Orientalist, but not to be classed with Dr. Green as a thoroughgoing conservative, and he exclaimed, with somewhat of impatience, at a man who would concede so much against traditional views and still draw back from the next step. Then I mentioned Dr. Green. "What, W. H. Green, of Princeton?" he said; "anything he says is entitled to respectful hearing," or some similar phrase. If I remember, Dr. Patton long ago in the *Presbyterian Review* used this phrase, "that the Presbyterian Church must not go into the Pentateuchal discussion as the advocate of a foregone conclusion." Dr. Green's conclusions are formed on solid evidence, out of a pure heart and with good conscience, and they compel homage even from the enemy.

These things have been gone over fully to-day, and I may, therefore, in this reminiscence meeting try to bring back a little more the impressions made upon us by this learned and devout doctor of the law, an Israelite, indeed, in whom is no guile. Semitic learning seems like a new world to the average collegian—for whom I may speak—coming up to this school of the prophets with his modicum of Latin and Greek—little Latin and less Greek, too often. It has been said to learn any new language is to add a new world to our knowledge, and certainly it is so with Hebrew. I remember talking with Dr. Purves (who was not a doctor then) in the old Seminary, soon after we came, and his speculating " how long it would take a fellow to learn to write a letter home in this language." Its strange characters, its crab-like progression, whereby one feels as if backing water across the page, are confusing to the beginner. Still more so is that peculiar motion by which one must weave the vowels from beneath into the consonantal framework above— one is so apt to drop a stitch. Dr. Green's mode of instruction made little provision for dropping stitches. It is hardly telling tales out of school to say—probably he knows it himself—that he was often called " Rabbi," and some even dared to speak of him as " Sinai." Not that he was harsh or unkind, but he was strict. The law was our schoolmaster. There was often a prevailing sense of shortcoming. We felt that in many *Points* —we offend all.

Since Dr. Patton this morning confessed his sin of ignorance of Hebrew I am moved to take refuge in his company and cry, *mea culpa.* Perhaps there are others in like case. Would it not be a good, practical outcome of to-day's Jubilee for us at least to make a good resolution that in vacations soon to come we will take Green's Hebrew Grammar with us? We will not find it hard to read. I know, for I took it last summer—I never expected to come to that, but I did—and found it delightful. It is full of himself, and what more could be said? After the first impression of class-rooms, strictness, delightful qualities come out. I shall never forget my surprise when I read that admirable little tractate, overflowing with keen satire, deliciously entitled "The Pentateuch Vindicated against the Aspersions of Bishop Colenso." It is, I hope, a title which posterity will not willingly let die, but preserve it amended by bracketing along with the bishop the names of some other learned Pundits, who still asperse the Pentateuch. It was my privilege to take a fourth year, studying with dear old Dr. Wistar Hodge in Biblical theology and with Dr. Green in Hengstenberg's Christology, talking familiarly with them both in the study; and when one comes to know Dr. Green thus his gentleness, sympathy, and goodness blend with his seriousness and make a very charming compound. I have even come to suspect other qualities in his Hebrew Grammar than those which appear on the surface. I should not be afraid to maintain the thesis as quite as defensible as some other results of the processes of higher criticism, that there is a subtle vein of humor running through the Grammar. It may have been unconscious on the part of its author. That distinguished scholar and antiquarian, Dr. Samuel Clemens, of the Hartford Theological Seminary (is he not?), so might, perhaps, issue a companion volume to that grammatical treatise intended for Portuguese youth, which he edited with such brilliant erudition some time ago, entitled "English as She Is Spoke." This might be called, "Hebrew as She Is Taught." It may need a "redacteur," but that the latest scholarship could easily supply. I might particularize, for instance, by referring to Dr. Green's treatment of that mysterious character, "Shv'a"—silent and vocal Shv'a. It is a mere echo of a sound, as though some patriarch had breathed a sigh upon the morning air, ages ago, and it still haunted the world. How deftly Dr. Green makes this ghost of a sound appear and disappear, like the ghost in "Hamlet." There is pathos in it, which is close to humor. Then there is Aleph — Aleph, the first letter of the Hebrew alphabet! Aleph in Dr. Green's Grammar appears not as a mere alphabetical character, but more as a living character—one of the *dramatis personæ* on the linguistic stage. Aleph is a weak letter. Dr. Green speaks as if he sympathized with the weakness of Aleph, perhaps smiled lovingly over it. I can fancy him feeling as Dr. Holmes did over " The Last Leaf : "

> " I know it is a sin.
> For me to sit and grin
> At him here."

As we read on in the grammar we can almost picture Aleph as an invalid, wrapped in fleecy robes against the wintry blast, or wheeled into the sunlight on some balmy Riviera coast.

But I can only suggest what you may pursue. One thing only let me say more. It has not been said to-day, but it is in every heart. We would all beg our beloved doctor to deal as gently with himself as he does with Aleph, remembering his own weakness, not of the spirit, but of the flesh. Let him not struggle too much with the radicals—but find some quiet spot where, to use the old phrase, he may "quiesce in Hholem," and gather new strength to win new victories for sound scholarship over pretentious pedantry, and sacred learning over irreverent vandalism. Meanwhile his revering pupils must try to follow in his footsteps. He has taught us to love the sacred things that he loved, and so to love better the God of all wisdom, love, and infinite grace.

THE HEAD OF THE FACULTY.

BY PROFESSOR WILLIAM M. PAXTON, D.D., LL.D.

My subject is Dr. Green as the Chairman of the Faculty, or, in other words, as President of the Seminary.

Dr. Green is certainly an ideal Chairman of the Faculty, for the reason that no man, probably, ever had such an ideal faculty over which to preside. They are the pick of the whole Church, elect men, elected by the board, elected by the General Assembly.

It is also the relation of these professors to Dr. Green that is so ideal. With one exception they are his students. They are his workmanship. He has made them, made them over his own last, and his sign and superscription are on them. I am the only exception, as I happened to be his fellow-student, he being a senior while I was a junior. As he had the reputation of being the most learned student in the Seminary, we were all taught to look up to him with the most profound veneration.

Thus much for what the magazines would call the lighter vein.

Now for a word—as our Methodist brethren sometimes say —of solemn, earnest testimony. Dr. Green's administration as President of this Seminary has been characterized by a success which has never been surpassed at any former period of our history. Under his guidance the Seminary has grown until its numbers have become almost burdensome. It has put on its beautiful garments, as any one can see who looks on Hodge Hall. It has grown in its curriculum until it is well-nigh perfect. And as the present company is always excepted, especially the speaker, it has grown in its Faculty by able and effective professors and teachers until the number has well-nigh doubled. This Faculty is perfectly united in thought, feeling, and affection. It would not be possible to find a group of scholarly men more perfectly harmonious upon all questions of religious faith and doctrine.

With all this, the Seminary has grown in the confidence of the Church and the approval of the public, for the reason that Princeton Seminary stands for something *positive* in religious belief and teaching, and the whole world sees this and approves.

The reason of all this success springs, in a great measure, from the strong personality and vigorous character of the man whom we this day delight to honor. The character of Dr. Green is made of blocks of solid granite. The storm of revision never shook it, and the mining and sapping of higher criticism never made him think for a moment that there was any danger that the ground upon which he stood would cave away under him.

Lord Bolingbroke, the leading English deist, said to a visitor: "I do not believe in a divine revelation, but those who do can best defend it on the principles of the doctrine of grace. Therefore I read John Calvin's 'Institutes,' because he stands upon the doctrine of grace. To say the truth," continues

Bolingbroke, "I have at times been almost persuaded to believe in a divine revelation on this view of things." Then turning to Dr. Church, a clergyman of the English Church, who had just said, "We don't think about such antiquated stuff. We teach the plain doctrines of virtue and morality, and have long laid aside these points about grace — turning to this clergyman, Bolingbroke continued: "There is one argument that has gone very far with me in behalf of the authenticity of the Bible, which is that any such thing as faith in the Bible now exists upon the earth, when its defence is committed to the care of such men as you, who pretend to believe it, and yet deny the only principles upon which it should be defended."

This is true to-day as it was then. There are ministers even in our own Church to-day who profess to believe the Bible, but who deny the principles of supernatural grace upon which it is best defended. But, thank God, there are men now who stand where John Calvin stood. It was his principles of supernatural grace that shook the doubts of Bolingbroke, and it is this Christian phalanx, at the head of which stands Dr. Green, that now shakes the doubts of speculative and revolutionary critics, and dissipates the fogs that have gathered over the fair face of Christianity. In this conflict Dr. Green has led the van. With an unfaltering courage he has always been ready to go forth in the name of God with his sling and stone to smite any Philistine who defies the armies of Israel.

It is for this reason that as the President of this Seminary we give him honor. He is so true himself that we believe it is the word of truth that he utters. He is so pure of heart that we feel sure, according to the promise, he sees God. He is so wise that, if it were not human to err, we might say he never makes a mistake. He is so just that his discipline is never doubted. And yet withal he is so kind, so considerate, so sympathetic, so generous, that we all — Faculty and students — this day do him honor, and give him, with the affection of our hearts, our loyal and loving obedience.

APPENDIX

TESTIMONIALS AND LETTERS OF REGRET FROM INSTITUTIONS OF LEARNING AND ASSOCIATIONS.

THE FACULTY OF PRINCETON THEOLOGICAL SEMINARY.

PRINCETON, N. J., May 5, 1896.

THE REVEREND WILLIAM HENRY GREEN, D.D., LL.D.

Dear Dr. Green : On this the fiftieth anniversary of your appointment to a place in the Faculty of which you are now the senior member and chairman, we, your colleagues, desire to add to those which you will receive from so many other sources the expression of our congratulations and best wishes, of our profound respect and warm affection.

We thank the Great Head of the Church for your long and eminent career and for the distinguished services which as teacher, preacher, and author you have been permitted to render to the truth and to the Church of God. We rejoice in the added distinction which your gifts and attainments and their high employment have conferred upon this venerable Seminary of sacred learning. All of us, except one, who was your fellow-student, have had the great honor and advantage of your instruction in the lecture-rooms of the Seminary ; and, with all your scholars, we are deeply indebted to you for having enlarged our knowledge and aided and stimulated our study of Holy Scripture, and for having confirmed our faith in its divine origin and supreme authority. Associated with you in the Faculty, we are your debtors, also, for your high example in daily life and in the discharge of official duty, for your wisdom in counsel, for your friendship and affection.

We pray that you will be continued long in life and health to bless your family, your friends, the community in which we live, the neighboring college, our Seminary, and the Church of Christ, and that you will enjoy always and abundantly the peace of God which passeth all understanding. We remain, dear Dr. Green, with veneration and with affection, very sincerely your friends,

> WILLIAM M. PAXTON,
> BENJAMIN BRECKINRIDGE WARFIELD,
> JOHN D. DAVIS,
> GEORGE T. PURVES,
> JOHN DEWITT,
> WILLIAM BRENTON GREENE, JR.,
> GEERHARDUS VOS,
> FRANCIS L. PATTON,
> CHALMERS MARTIN.

FROM THE STUDENTS OF PRINCETON SEMINARY.

On the occasion of the fiftieth anniversary of Dr. William Henry Green's entrance upon his duties in Princeton Theological Seminary, we, who are now his students, wish to give expression to the affection and esteem in which we hold him. We have been helped by his work for us in the class-room. We have been deeply moved by his earnest spiritual addresses. Above all, his warm personal interest in each one of us, his simple, right life, his humble piety and Christian walk have been to us a constant inspiration in the service of Christ, his Lord, and ours.

Signed by all the students in the Seminary, session of 1895-96.

ACTION OF THE FACULTY OF PRINCETON COLLEGE.

The Faculty tender their cordial congratulations to the authorities of the Theological Seminary and to Dr. Green on the occasion of the fiftieth anniversary of his appointment as Instructor in the Seminary. During this long period of service he has pursued the vocation of a scholar and teacher not only with enthusiasm, fidelity, and industry, but with a modesty, contentment, and success demanding the most generous recognition. The academic profession is indebted to him for such an example of its highest virtues.

In an age when the cause of Semitic scholarship and Biblical learning has awakened new zeal and research he has kept pace with its progress, and has enriched it with valuable works, which are replete with solid erudition and cogent argument. The judgment of competent critics abroad, as well as of pupils and colleagues at home, has placed him in the front rank of Hebrew scholars.

As an advocate of the Higher Criticism, his eminent learning has been ennobled by intelligent reverence for the Holy Scriptures and by true spiritual discernment in connection with that linguistic tact, literary skill, and historical research which are requisite in the study of all ancient literature. The result is that he has not disturbed the faith of the unlearned, while commanding the respect of scholars.

Although his professional work has been confined to the Theological Seminary, the College has had the constant benefit of his counsel in the Board of Trustees; the Faculty has found in him an appreciative co-worker in promoting the higher education; and the whole academic body has enjoyed the polished and fervent discourses which he has occasionally preached in the chapel. His influence has thus been widely extended beyond the sphere of his sacred studies.

Above all the rewards and honors of scholarship, he is now distinguished by a ripe Christian character, in which the academic laurel appears entwined with that wreath that fadeth not away. "Serus in cœlum redeat."

Attest :   HENRY CLAY CAMERON,
                 Clerk of Faculty.

ACTION OF THE PRESBYTERY OF NEW BRUNSWICK.

TO THE REV. WILLIAM H. GREEN, D.D., LL.D.

Beloved and Reverend Sir : The Presbytery of New Brunswick, ministers and ruling elders alike, join with other ecclesiastical organizations and with a multitude of our Christian brethren throughout this and other lands in affectionate and hearty congratulations on the fiftieth anniversary of your appointment as Instructor in the Theological Seminary at Princeton. For nearly fifty years you have been identified with this Presbytery, and the majority of the ministers now connected therewith have known you not only as a co-presbyter, but as their revered, honored, and beloved teacher, to whom they owe a debt of gratitude for the prominent part you have had in preparing them for their life-work and in furnishing them so large a portion of the equipment used as preachers of the Word.

We all join in the high estimate so many thoughtful men throughout the Church have placed upon the contributions you have made to biblical criticism, Semitic scholarship, and related branches of learning, as evinced by articles from your pen in our periodical literature and by the scholarly books you have given to the world. We have admired you and have been edified by you as a preacher of the Word, and we especially assure you of our grateful appreciation of you as a member of the same Presbytery with us. Your Christian courtesy, your evident interest in all that pertains to the welfare of our churches, your wise counsels, your uniform kindness, have all combined to win for you a warm place in our regard and to call forth our veneration for your personal character and worth. We give thanks to God for your long, useful, and busy life as an instructor of instructors, and for the influence you have exerted in behalf of the purity and authority of revealed truth as given to us in the Bible.

Our united prayer is that you may yet for many years be spared to your family, to this Presbytery, to the Seminary, and to the Church at large, and that you may be enabled still to do successful work for the cause of truth and righteousness. May the grace of the Great Teacher and the comforts of the Holy Ghost be yours in rich abundance, till you shall enter upon the glorious reward of those who have fought a good fight, and have finished their course, and have kept the faith.

In behalf of the Presbytery :

SAMUEL M. STUDDIFORD,
ABRAHAM GOSMAN,
HENRY C. CAMERON, *Committee.*
FRANK L. JANEWAY,
WILLIAM J. OWENS,

THE PRESBYTERIAN CHURCH OF ALLENTOWN, N. J.

Whereas, The fiftieth anniversary of the professorate of the Rev. William H. Green, D.D., LL.D., in the Theological Seminary at Princeton is to be observed on Tuesday, May 5th ; and

Whereas, The Rev. Dr. Green was for a time, when a lad, a member, with his father's family, of this congregation ;

Resolved, That we, the people of the Presbyterian Church at Allentown, N. J., tender to Dr. Green our congratulations and rejoice with gratitude to our Lord because of his high attainment as a scholar, and in view of his very eminent service for the Presbyterian Church and the kingdom of God.

Resolved, also, That this resolution be signed by the clerk of the session, Mr. Henry R. Taylor, and forwarded to Dr. Green by the pastor, Rev. George Swain.

[Signed] HENRY R. TAYLOR,
Clerk of Session.

ALLENTOWN, N. J., May 3, 1896.

THE PRESBYTERY OF PHILADELPHIA.

The Presbytery of Philadelphia extends its most hearty congratulations to the Rev. William Henry Green, D.D., LL.D., our former co-presbyter, on the occasion of the fiftieth anniversary of his connection with Princeton Theological Seminary as teacher of Old Testament and Oriental Literature, expressing at the same time the hope and prayer that he may be spared for many years to continue that important work, for the prosecution of which he has been so richly endowed by the Head of the Church, and in which he has made such high attainment as to deservedly win international reputation.

ANDREW JACKSON SULLIVAN,
Moderator.

W. W. RICE, *Stated Clerk.*
ROBERT HUNTER, *Permanent Clerk.*

Adopted unanimously by a rising vote. May 4, 1896. R. H.

THE PRESBYTERIAN MINISTERIAL ASSOCIATION OF PHILADELPHIA AND VICINITY.

The following paper was adopted May 4, 1896, by the Presbyterian Ministerial Association of Philadelphia and Vicinity, and directed to be presented to Professor William Henry Green on the occasion of the fiftieth anniversary of his professorship in Princeton Theological Seminary by a committee consisting of Rev. Thomas Murphy, D.D., Rev. J. Addison Henry, D.D., and Rev. Thomas A. Hoyt, D.D.

Among all the favored men of the present day who have been raised up by the Lord for the honor of our Church, the defence of His cause, and the glory of His name, there is none more worthy of a high place in public estimation than Professor W. H. Green, of Princeton Theological Seminary. We do not use language of exaggeration, but "words of truth and soberness," in assigning him a lofty position on the roll of Christian scholarship. We might attempt to depict the great excellence of his character, which has impressed itself on the many hundreds of young men in whose training for the sacred ministry he has taken so conspicuous a part. His own personal modesty is such that other pens than his own must do this, but we rejoice that many others are doing it justly and lovingly. It is probable that no living man has rendered more valuable services than Dr. Green in the sphere of oriental learning, by his grammar of the Hebrew language, his revised version of a portion of the Old

Testament, and his masterly defence of important parts of the Sacred Scriptures. In addition to these we cannot fail to mention his invaluable work as a teacher of theology, who has never faltered in the soundness of his views. In celebrating the jubilee of such a professor our Church does honor to herself and to the cause of which for half a century he has been a noble representative. He is pre-eminently a learned, great, and a good man, combining the rare qualities of a ripe scholar and a humble Christian. It will long be regarded as a distinction to have been trained in the theological school of which he is so conspicuous an ornament.

THE MINISTERS' ASSOCIATION OF BALTIMORE.

The Ministers' Association of Baltimore City, consisting of the pastors of the Presbyterian, Reformed, and Congregational Churches, beg to express their congratulations to the Directors of Princeton Theological Seminary and to Professor William Henry Green, on the completion of his fiftieth year of instruction. The Church and the world have recognized his peculiar gifts and eminent services in his department in interpreting and vindicating the authority and integrity of the Holy Scriptures, in which appreciation this association cordially joins and expresses the hope that he may be long spared to continue his labors.
Signed for the Committee:
JOSEPH T. SMITH,
JOHN P. CAMPBELL,
E. E. WEAVER.

The above resolution was unanimously adopted at the meeting of the Association, April 27, 1896.
For the Committee :
JOHN P. CAMPBELL.
BALTIMORE, MD., April 28, 1896.

ALLIANCE OF THE REFORMED CHURCHES.

PHILADELPHIA, PA., May 4, 1896.
TO THE FACULTY OF THE PRINCETON THEOLOGICAL SEMINARY.
Dear Brethren: The Western Section of the Commission of this Alliance, in session at Philadelphia, Pa., April 26, 1896, having had brought to their attention the fact that the semi-centennial of the Rev. William Henry Green, D.D., LL.D., Professor of Oriental and Old Testament

APPENDIX 95

Literature in the Seminary, was about to be celebrated, in order to give expression to the sentiments of high esteem and regard cherished by the Churches represented in the Alliance for the Rev. Dr. Green, by resolution, duly adopted, appointed a delegation to be present at the semi-centennial exercise. This delegation consists of the Rev. William H. Roberts, D.D., LL.D., Chairman of the Section and President of the Alliance; the Rev. D. J. Burrell, D.D., of the Collegiate Reformed Church, New York City; the Rev. David Steele, D.D., Professor in the Reformed Theological Seminary, Philadelphia, Pa.; the Rev. David Waters, D.D., of the Reformed Dutch Church; the Rev. W. Barr, D.D., Secretary of the Board of Foreign Missions of the United Presbyterian Church; and the Rev. James I. Good, D.D., Professor in the German Reformed College, at Reading, Pa.

Tendering to you our warm congratulations upon this auspicious anniversary, I am, in behalf of the Alliance,
Yours cordially,
WILLIAM HENRY ROBERTS.

TELEGRAM FROM THE CONVENTION OF THE PROTESTANT EPISCOPAL DIOCESE OF NEW JERSEY.

ELIZABETH, N. J., May 5, 1896.

The Convention of the Diocese of New Jersey sends its congratulations to the Rev. Dr. William Henry Green upon the happy anniversary which is this day being observed in Princeton, and expresses its grateful appreciation of the eminent service he has rendered the entire world in the Department of Old Testament Criticism and Interpretation.

ELVIN K. SMITH,
Secretary.

AUBURN THEOLOGICAL SEMINARY.

AUBURN, N. Y., May 1, 1896.

REV. AND DEAR SIR:

The Faculty of the Theological Seminary of Auburn, in the State of New York, desire most cordially to acknowledge the courtesy of the invitation to be present at the celebration of the fiftieth anniversary of the appointment of Professor William Henry Green as an Instructor in the Seminary.

The pressure of engagements connected with the closing exercise of our own Seminary forbids a general acceptance. We are grateful, however, to be represented by our senior professor, who is also a co-laborer with Dr. Green in the department of Old Testament Literature, and who will be able to express personally our congratulation and our rejoicing with you in this interesting anniversary. We desire as a body to express our appreciation of the noble labors of Professor Green, the high ideals of scholarship and of Christian living which he has illustrated in these long years of consecrated devotion to the work to which God early called him, and of the honor which he has reflected upon our Church and upon American scholarship. We unite with you in our prayer to the Head of the Church that he may long be spared to bring forth fruit in old age to the glory of God and to the advancement of sound faith and Biblical learning. On behalf of the Faculty, I have the honor to be

Yours most respectfully,

TIMOTHY G. DARLING,
Clerk.

DANVILLE THEOLOGICAL SEMINARY.

DANVILLE, KY., April 11, 1896.

MY DEAR SIR:

I have held the invitation to attend the fiftieth anniversary of Dr. Green's appointment to service in Princeton Seminary, hoping to find my way clear to attend. I admire and love Dr. Green very sincerely, and would be most happy to express my interest by attending that service; but the recent death of our loved and venerated Dr. Yerkes makes it incumbent on me to be here the week of the service at Princeton. So I am obliged to decline.

Very truly yours,

J. M. WORRALL.

THE GERMAN PRESBYTERIAN THEOLOGICAL SCHOOL OF THE NORTHWEST.

DUBUQUE, IA., April 9, 1896.

DEAR BROTHER:

Our Faculty desired me to express through you its appreciation of the honor conferred by your committee in the invitation given to attend the celebration of the fiftieth anniversary of the appointment of Dr. William Henry Green as an Instructor in the Seminary. This Faculty is in hearty sympathy with the purpose of this celebration and regrets the fact that none of its members can be present on that great occasion. Every member of this Faculty cherishes the highest regard for the great and good Doctor and would have been much pleased to give visible expression of this by being present at the celebration on the fifth proximo.

On behalf of the Faculty :
ADAM MCCLELLAND,
Chairman.

THE SAN FRANCISCO THEOLOGICAL SEMINARY.

SAN ANSELMO, CAL., April 2, 1896.
DEAR BROTHER :

Our Faculty have received the invitation to attend the fiftieth anniversary of Dr. William Henry Green's connection with Princeton Seminary as an Instructor. Every member of the Faculty would esteem it a great privilege and honor to be present on an occasion of so much interest to our entire Church. But distance will prevent the attendance of any of our number. We would like, however, to unite in the great chorus of congratulations which will be offered at this time. We congratulate Princeton Seminary that it has enjoyed for half a century the services of so eminent a scholar, so efficient a teacher, and so humble and modest a follower of Jesus Christ. We congratulate the Presbyterian Church that it has so long profited by the services of one who is admitted to be one of the most distinguished divines and one of the most eminent Biblical scholars in the world. Please express to Dr. Green our great affection for him, for, though some of us have never been intimately associated with him, we have long since learned to love him. Also express the hope that he may be spared much longer to be what he has so long been, a teacher of ministers, an example to believers, and a defender of the faith.

On behalf of the Faculty :
THOMAS F. DAY,
Chairman,
WARREN H. LANDON,
Clerk.

UNION THEOLOGICAL SEMINARY, NEW YORK CITY.

The Faculty of the Union Theological Seminary acknowledge the courtesy of the invitation of the Theological Seminary at Princeton for the 5th of May, which we regret we are unable to accept.

Very truly yours,
FRANCIS BROWN,
Secretary of Faculty.

THE RICHMOND THEOLOGICAL SEMINARY.

RICHMOND, VA., March 26, 1896.

DEAR SIR:

Your kind invitation to be present at the fiftieth anniversary of the appointment of Professor Green is at hand. I exceedingly regret that I cannot be present on that occasion. Please tender my hearty congratulations to Dr. Green, the distinguished teacher, whose name is a household word among the Biblical scholars of the nineteenth century, and whose influence in the cause of sacred learning is felt among all the nations of the earth and the far-off islands of the sea.

Respectfully yours,
C. H. COREY,
President.

UNION THEOLOGICAL SEMINARY, VIRGINIA.

HAMPDEN-SIDNEY, VA., March 28, 1896.

DEAR BROTHER:

In behalf of the Faculty of Union Theological Seminary in Virginia, I beg to acknowledge with thanks your kind invitation to attend the celebration of the fiftieth anniversary of the appointment of Professor William Henry Green as an Instructor in the Theological Seminary of the Presbyterian Church in the U. S. A., at Princeton, N. J.

Recognizing the fact that the occasion is one worthy of being commemorated, it is a matter of genuine regret that our own Institution, having so much in common with yours, cannot be represented in person. It would, indeed, be a privilege to do honor to one so deserving of honor, and to join in thanksgiving to God for the services rendered by this dauntless soldier of the cross, who has so long stood in the breach, and because of whom so many of the friends of the truth have had occasion to thank God and take courage. All honor to this venerable defender of the faith, and may his bow long abide in strength, to the confusion of all enemies of the truth and to the comfort of its friends. With the heartiest congratulations.

Yours very sincerely,
T. R. ENGLISH,
Clerk of the Faculty.

APPENDIX 99

ERSKINE THEOLOGICAL SEMINARY.

Due West, S. C., April 2, 1896.

Whereas, The Theological Seminary of Princeton, N. J., has extended an invitation to Erskine Theological Seminary to be present at the semi-centennial celebration of the professorship of William Henry Green, D.D., LL.D.; therefore

Resolved, By the Faculty and students of Erskine Theological Seminary, that we express our grateful appreciation of the kind invitation, and beg to unite in the congratulations of the occasion to one who by his piety and learning is rightly recognized as one of the ablest representatives of Biblical scholarship in this country; and who by his unswerving defence of the truth has made the whole Church his debtor.

W. L. Pressly,
President.

THE ALLEGHENY THEOLOGICAL SEMINARY.

March 25, 1896.

Dear Brother :

We are pleased to have your invitation to the celebration of the fiftieth anniversary of the introduction of Professor William Henry Green into the corps of instructors of Princeton Theological Seminary.

No man more deserves recognition at the hands of his Church and of all the Churches than Professor Green. He has been and is a tower of strength to the cause of Christian learning upon this continent. His work is even increasingly valuable as the Old Testament is more critically examined. The Church is everywhere thankful that such a man has been raised up for the defence of the truth. Please convey our good wishes to him. We trust that the occasion will prove a very enjoyable one.

I am very truly yours, for the Faculty :

J. A. Grier.

REFORMED PRESBYTERIAN THEOLOGICAL SEMINARY, ALLEGHENY, PA.

Allegheny, Pa., May 4, 1896.

Dear Sir :

We rejoice with you all in the celebration this week on account of the long service Dr. William Henry Green has been enabled to render to

Princeton Seminary. This has been a service to which the whole Church of Christ, by reason of his devotion to the study of the Scriptures, his instruction of so many ministers of the Word of God, and his constant defence of its integrity and authority.
Yours in the service of Christ,
D. B. WILLSON.

AUGSBURG SEMINARY (LUTHERAN).

MINNEAPOLIS, MINN., March 26, 1896.

The kind invitation to the celebration on May 5th at the fiftieth anniversary of the appointment of Professor W. H. Green is duly received. As Augsburg Seminary cannot be represented on this occasion, we beg to send our congratulations. May the blessing of our Lord rest on the Seminary and its teachers and students!
In behalf of Augsburg Seminary :
GEORGE SVENDRUP,
President.

BANGOR THEOLOGICAL SEMINARY.

BANGOR, ME., March 26, 1896.
DEAR SIR :
I am appointed by the Faculty of the Bangor Theological Seminary to respond to the invitation to attend the Jubilee of Dr. Green's connection with Princeton Theological Seminary. This institution sends its greetings and congratulations to Princeton Seminary and to Dr. Green, and wishes many years of usefulness to the reverend professor, whose devotion to the institution you will soon acknowledge. The Faculty of Bangor also send thanks for the invitation, but regret inability to attend, inasmuch as our own duties will not permit our absence so near the end of the academic year.
For the Faculty :
GEORGE W. GILMORE.

THE THEOLOGICAL FACULTY OF BOSTON UNIVERSITY.

March 31, 1896.
REVEREND AND DEAR SIR :
On behalf of the Theological Faculty of Boston University, the undersigned returns sincere thanks to the authorities of Princeton Theological Seminary for their kind invitation to share in the approaching Jubilaeum.

The occasion is one of interest to all American scholars and particularly to all evangelical theological seminaries. But for the expected absence of our Dean from home and possibly of one or two other members of our Faculty the whole month, we should doubtless appoint a representative to be present at the celebration. As it is, we send our most cordial congratulations to your honored Seminary and our sincere wishes that yet other fruitful years may be added to the life of the colleague whom we all so highly honor.

Fraternally yours,
WILLIAM F. WARREN.

CHICAGO THEOLOGICAL SEMINARY.

March 31, 1896.

Our Faculty were much gratified to receive the invitation to be present at the fiftieth anniversary of Dr. Green's appointment as teacher in Princeton Theological Seminary. I doubt if any of us will be able to attend in person, but we will all be there in spirit and rejoice in the recognition of great learning, ability, devotion to truth, and personal piety, which will be given in the honors paid Professor Green. *Nomen clarum et venerabile!* May every blessing attend him and the noble institution which he so worthily represents. In behalf of the Faculty.

Very truly yours,
H. M. SCOTT,
Secretary.

THE SCHOOL OF THEOLOGY OF DE PAUW UNIVERSITY.

GREENCASTLE, IND., March 25, 1896.

DEAR SIR:

I have received your very kind invitation to the celebration of the fiftieth anniversary of the appointment of Professor William Henry Green. I am very sorry that my engagements make it impossible for me to be present. I hold Dr. Green in the most profound honor and esteem. He has done an eminently great work for the cause of theological education. He deserves a testimonial from the entire nation in recognition of his great services. I trust the occasion will prove very gratifying to all concerned. If a newspaper account is published, I shall esteem it a great pleasure to receive a copy, and will gladly pay the expenses of the same.

Very cordially,
H. A. GOBIN,
Dean of School of Theology and Acting President.

DREW THEOLOGICAL SEMINARY.

MADISON, N. J., April 13, 1896.

TO THE THEOLOGICAL SEMINARY OF THE PRESBYTERIAN CHURCH AT PRINCETON, N. J. :

The Faculty of Drew Theological Seminary of the Methodist Episcopal Church beg to acknowledge with thanks the kind invitation with which you have honored us to be present at the celebration of the fiftieth anniversary of the appointment of Professor William Henry Green as an Instructor in the Seminary.

Your celebration comes at the time when the General Conference of our Church is in session, and as some of our Faculty will be members of that body and the others will be in Europe, we greatly regret that we cannot be personally represented on that important occasion. We will be with you, however, in spirit, and join most heartily in every tribute of reverence and affection for the eminent professor, scholar, and author who has rendered such valuable service not only to the Presbyterian Church, but to the whole Christian world. Professor Green's long period of usefulness in the institution which he has served with such distinguished ability has made an abiding impression on the age, and his writings have contributed alike to the advancement of Biblical scholarship and to the defence of the sacred Scriptures.

We unite in the profoundest respect for Dr. Green and in sincerest congratulations to the Seminary which has so long had the privilege of having his name associated with it. Wishing for you a most delightful and successful occasion, I am, on behalf of the Faculty,

Very sincerely yours,

HENRY A. BUTTZ.

THE THEOLOGICAL SEMINARY OF THE EVANGELICAL LUTHERAN CHURCH OF OHIO AND ADJACENT STATES.

The Theological Seminary of the Evangelical Lutheran Synod of Ohio and Adjacent States sends greeting to the Theological Seminary of the Presbyterian Church in the United States, and recognizing the eminent services rendered by Dr. William Henry Green to the cause of Christianity, congratulates him and the Seminary which he has so long and so ably served upon the fiftieth anniversary of his professorship, with the Faculty's regrets that they are unable to be personally represented at the coming celebration.

COLUMBUS, O., March 31, 1896.

GAMMON THEOLOGICAL SEMINARY.

ATLANTA, GA., April 26, 1896.

REVEREND AND DEAR SIR :

We beg to acknowledge with sincere thanks the invitation to be present at the celebration of the fiftieth anniversary of the appointment of Professor William H. Green as Instructor in your noble institution. We very much regret the inability of our Seminary to have a representative with you on that occasion.

We remember with especial pleasure a visit which Dr. Green was kind enough to pay to us several years ago, and the shelves of our library bear witness to the generous spirit of this noble scholar and friend of humanity. He was kind enough to send us a set of his publications. With congratulations and regards, we remain,

Fraternally and truly yours,

W. P. THIRKIELD,
President.

GARRETT BIBLICAL INSTITUTE.

The Faculty of Garrett Biblical Institute, at Evanston, Ill., express their thanks to the Princeton Theological Seminary for the honor of an invitation to the celebration of Professor Green's fiftieth anniversary, and regret exceedingly that duties connected with commencement week in Evanston and with the session of the General Conference of the Methodist Episcopal Church at Cleveland, O., render it impossible for any representation of the Evanston Seminary to be present at the celebration. The Faculty of the Institute are happy to have this opportunity to express their high appreciation of the noble character and distinguished services of Professor Green, and to send to Princeton Seminary their congratulations and fraternal greetings.

Signed for the Faculty :

CHARLES J. LITTLE, *President.*
CHARLES F. BRADLY, *Secretary.*

EVANSTON, ILL., April 27, 1896.

שלם רב לאהבי תורתך

HEBREW UNION COLLEGE.

CINCINNATI, O., May, 1896.

לכבוד החכם המפ׳אר
פְּרוֹפֶסָר וִילְיַם הָנְרִי גְרִין בעיר פְּרִינְסֶטָן

אדוננו הנכבד:

בְּשׂוֹרָה בָאָה אלינו כי קרבה לך שְׁנַת יובל שְׁנַת החמשים שנה
מיום הוקמת עַל להיות מורה בבית הַלְּמּוּדִים אשר נודע בשם
Princeton Theological Seminary.

נכבדות יְדָבָּר בך ביום היובל הזה ומקרוב ומרחוק יבאו אליך
תלמידיך והבריך ורעיך וברכות יְעַטְרוּ את המורה הזקן והנהדר:
גם אֲנַחְנוּ המורים בבית המדרש אשר לנו פה בעירנו נִקְרָא
נקראנו לבא למקום שְׁבְּתֶךָ להתערב בשמחת יום חגך ולתת כבוד לאיש
אשר יאתה לו התהלה: אך יען רחוק ממנו המקום לא נוכל להראות
את פניך לכן ממרחקים נזכרך ונשלח אליך את דברי האגרת הזאת
דברי שלום וברכה כי ידענו את גדל ערכך יאת פעלתך הָרַבָּה והטוּבה
גם בתורת פיך גם בספריך היקרים אשר הוצאת לאור לפרוש אור
חכמתך על הַשָּׂפָה העבריה ועל סִפְרֵי הַקֹּדֶשׁ: ישלם אלהים פעלך
ותהי מַשְׂכֻּרְתֶּךָ שְׁלֵמָה מֵעִם אדון עולם: יֹסֶף עוד שָׁנִים על שְׁנוֹתֶיךָ
ותעמד גם בגבורת על משמרתך ועוד תנוב בשֵׂיבָה טובה וברוכה:
דברי עבדיך מכבדיך הטורים בבית המדרש פה בעירנו:

The President and the Faculty of the Hebrew Union College.

ISAAC M. WISE,
President H. U. C.

DR. M. MIELZINER,
Secretary pro tem.

THE MISSION HOUSE OF THE REFORMED CHURCH IN THE UNITED STATES OF AMERICA.

To the Theological Seminary of the Presbyterian Church in the United States of North America, at Princeton, N. J.

GREETING.

We gratefully acknowledge the receipt of an invitation to be present at the celebration of the fiftieth anniversary of Professor William Henry Green as an Instructor in this Seminary. Regretting our inability to be present in person, we would, nevertheless, extend our most cordial congratulations to the Seminary and to Professor Green, who, by the providence of our Heavenly Father, has been enabled so long to fill the useful and honorable office of a professor of theology. We acknowledge the eminent services which Dr. Green has rendered not only to the Presbyterian Church, but by his literary labors to the Christian Church in general ; and we pray God still to protect and bless him and to crown the evening of his life with the peace which passeth all understanding.

Given at Franklin, Wis., March 27, 1896.
H. A. Muehlmeir, *President*,
H. A. Muir, *Secretary*,
J. Van Haagen,
J. Glaubertz,
Frank Grether,
J. W. Grosshuesch,
D. S. Hagenmeyer,
Edward Hentz,

The Faculty of the Mission House of the Reformed
Church in the United States.

THEOLOGICAL SEMINARY OF THE (LUTHERAN) UNITED SYNOD, NEWBERRY, S. C.

Newberry, S. C., March 27, 1896.

Dear Sir :

I take great pleasure in acknowledging with thanks the receipt of the invitation of the Theological Seminary at Princeton to be present at the anniversary celebration in honor of Dr. William Henry Green. It will not be possible, I regret to say, for me to be present on the notable occasion. But I may at least have the pleasure of expressing here in a sentence or two the high appreciation I have of the very eminent services of Dr. Green. The anniversary of so extraordinarily long and able a career as an instructor and theologian is an event not only in the history of Princeton Seminary, but of theological education the world over. The services of Dr. Green to the cause of conservative Biblical scholarship were never more valuable than in recent years, and it almost appears as if his learning and ability could be least of all spared at the present time, when his distinguished career is drawing to so glorious a close.

May many years of usefulness still be added to the fifty that have passed and may God crown the evening of life for His distinguished servant with His peace.

Very respectfully yours,
A. G. VOIGT,
Senior Professor.

NEWTON THEOLOGICAL INSTITUTE.

NEWTON CENTER, MASS., May 2, 1896.

MY DEAR DR. GREEN:

I have been requested by my colleagues in the Faculty of the Newton Theological Institution to represent them, either in person or by letter, at the fiftieth anniversary of your work as a teacher in Princeton. Until two days ago I entertained a hope of being able to be in Princeton on the 5th, that I might have the pleasure of seeing you again with the other distinguished scholars who will be there to pay you deserved honor. But I regret to find that pressing duties will prevent my leaving Newton at that time. The only thing, therefore, which I can do in fulfilment of the wishes of my associates is to assure you by letter of our high appreciation of your truly eminent and faithful service of Christ in the defence and interpretation of the Old Testament. This I do with all my heart. For a quarter of a century I have looked upon your writings as invaluable. Their learning, lucidness, and cogency have always commanded respect. Their unswerving defence of the authenticity and integrity of the Pentateuch has sustained the faith and courage of many. To them I reckon myself a debtor for a large amount of instruction, and from them as well as from personal intercourse with yourself in my own home I have learned to think of you always as an earnest and powerful defender of revealed truth.

With multitudes who reverence "the oracles of God" I cherish the hope that your work as a living interpreter may yet continue many years, but at the same time the assurance that if that form of your service should end to-morrow, your work in other forms would go on to the end of time.

In behalf of my associates, I am with great respect,

Most cordially yours,
ALVAH HOVEY,
President Newton Theological Institute.

OBERLIN THEOLOGICAL SEMINARY.

OBERLIN, O., April 8, 1896.

DEAR SIR:

I have the honor, on behalf of the Faculty of Oberlin Theological Seminary, to acknowledge the receipt of your invitation to participate in the celebration of the fiftieth anniversary of the appointment of Professor William Henry Green as an Instructor in Princeton Seminary.

It would give us great pleasure to be represented on that occasion, and to do honor to one so eminent for his services to Biblical learning, but the distance and the fact that our own anniversary falls in the same week will make it impossible.

With best wishes for the prosperity of the Seminary, believe me,
Fraternally yours,
W. G. BALLENTINE,
President.

PAYNE THEOLOGICAL SEMINARY.

WILBERFORCE, O., April 28, 1896.

DEAR SIR:

The Faculty of Payne Theological Seminary desire to acknowledge with thanks the invitation extended them, and regret to reply that, owing to the absence of some professors and the consequent arrangement of work, acceptance is not possible. They would offer to the Faculty of Princeton Seminary hearty congratulations and assurances of high esteem.

Yours most sincerely,
W. L. SCARBOROUGH,
Secretary.

DIVINITY SCHOOL OF THE PROTESTANT EPISCOPAL CHURCH IN PHILADELPHIA.

PHILADELPHIA, PA., May 4, 1896.

REVEREND AND DEAR SIR:

On behalf of the Faculty of this divinity school, I beg leave to express our thanks for the courteous invitation to attend the celebration of Professor Green's anniversary and our regrets that our duties here will not allow any of us to be present. Not only are all our lectures still in course, but also our Diocesan Convention is to be in session, and we are required to attend that. We join with all the Church in doing honor to Dr. Green's

long and important services to the cause of sound learning, and would be glad to evince our interest in the anniversary by personal attendance, if it were not that we are under the necessity of remaining at our own post of duty. With sincere fraternal greeting, I am,
Faithfully yours,
EDWARD T. BARTLETT.

THEOLOGICAL SEMINARY OF THE REFORMED PRESBYTERIAN CHURCH AT PHILADELPHIA.

PHILADELPHIA, PA., May 5, 1896.

TO PROFESSOR WILLIAM HENRY GREEN, D.D., LL.D. :

The undersigned, members of the Faculty of the Theological Seminary of the General Synod of the Reformed Presbyterian Church in North America, organized anno Domini 1807, and located in Philadelphia, Pa., take pleasure in sending their congratulations to you upon the occasion of your semi-centennial as Professor of Hebrew and Oriental Literature in Princeton Theological Seminary. As teachers in one of the schools of the prophets we send you this tribute of affection and respect, recognizing in you the profound thinker, the ripe scholar, and, above all, the peerless defender of all that is sacred and divine in the origin, unity, inspiration, and infallibility of the Holy Scriptures.

DAVID STEELE, *Professor of Doctrinal Theology*,
MATTHEW GAILEY, *Professor of Hebrew, Old Testament Literature and Church History*,
JAMES Y. BOICE, *Professor of New Testament Greek, Homiletics and Pastoral Theology*.

THE DIVINITY SCHOOL OF TUFTS COLLEGE.

TUFTS COLLEGE, MASS., March 25, 1896.

Professor Charles H. Leonard, Dean of the Divinity School of this College, thanks the Theological Seminary of the Presbyterian Church in the United States for the kind invitation to be present at the celebration of the fiftieth anniversary of the appointment of Professor William Henry Green as an Instructor in the Seminary, and deeply regrets that he cannot be present on an occasion when a great school honors a gifted and faithful teacher.

STILLMAN INSTITUTE.

TUSCALOOSA, ALA., April 7, 1896.

DEAR SIR AND BROTHER :

Your kind invitation to the Institute for Training Colored Ministers, now Stillman Institute, to attend the fiftieth anniversary of the appointment of Dr. Green as an Instructor in Princeton Seminary has been duly received. We highly appreciate the honor of your invitation, but circumstances prevent our acceptance of it. May I be allowed to say that, in common with all orthodox Christians throughout the world, we gladly enter into the spirit of this occasion, congratulating the venerable and holy Seminary and the great Professor upon this golden wedding, and praying that they may still bring forth fruit in their old age.

Your brother in Christ,

A. L. PHILLIPS,
Superintendent.

THE SCHOOL OF THEOLOGY OF URSINUS COLLEGE.

COLLEGEVILLE, PA., April 30, 1896.

TO THE FACULTY OF PRINCETON THEOLOGICAL SEMINARY:

Dear Brethren: The Faculty of the School of Theology of Ursinus College desire to place on record a minute of their high appreciation of the labors and character of the Rev. Professor William Henry Green, D.D., LL.D., of Princeton Theological Seminary, for his extensive scholarship, his noble defence of the old faith against the rationalistic criticism of the Scriptures, his Christian courtesy to his opponents, and the spirituality of his personal influence on his students. They congratulate him on his semi-centennial of service, and pray that his life may long be spared to continue his work as a teacher and a defender of the truth. They regret that, owing to the fact that the public examinations and commencement of our School of Theology take place on Tuesday, May 5th, they are not able to be represented at the semi-centennial exercises at Princeton, but assure him and his associates in the Faculty of our sincerest sympathy and heartiest congratulations.

JAMES I. GOOD, *Dean of School of Theology*,
WILLIAM HINKE, *Instructor in Hebrew and
Old Testament Theology.*

WARTBURG SEMINARY OF THE EVANGELICAL LUTHERAN SYNOD OF IOWA.

DUBUQUE, Ia., May 1, 1896.

SEINER HOCHWÜRDEN,
HERRN DR. TH. W. H. GREEN, PRINCETON, N. J.

Hochwürdiger Herr Doctor : Es ist mir leider versagt, bei Ihrer Jubelfeier am 5 May in Princeton anwesend zu sein und Ihnen meine und meiner Collegen Segenswünsche persönlich darzubringen. Gestatten Sie mir, dies wenigstens mit diesen Zeilen zu thun. Wir verehren in Ihnen den treuen Zeugen, der in einer Zeit zunehmenden Abfalles sich nicht schämt, zum Worte der Offenbarung sich zu bekennen und den Reichthum seines Wissens und die Kraft seines Geistes zur Vertheidigung des alten Glaubens wider die Blendwerke der falschberühmten modernen Kritik und Wissenschaft verwendet. Sie sind dadurch zahllosen Christenherzen —auch unter uns Deutschen—zum Segen und zur Stärkung geworden. Darum treibt uns auch das Herz, an Ihrem Jubelfeste dies mit innigem Danke zu bekennen und mit allen Ihren Freunden Gott zu preisen, dass er Ihnen verliehen hat Ihr gesegnetes Wirken so lange fort zu setzen. Er sei selber Ihr Lohn.

In tiefer Verehrung.

SIGMUND FRITSCHEL, D.D.,
Präsident des ev. luth. Predigerseminars,
Wartburg.

WESTERN THEOLOGICAL SEMINARY OF THE REFORMED (DUTCH) CHURCH IN AMERICA.

HOLLAND, MICH., April 10, 1896

MY DEAR BROTHER :

I am requested by our Theological Faculty to acknowledge the receipt of your kind invitation to attend the celebration of Professor Green's appointment as Instructor in your Seminary. We desire to accept it with thanks, although our distance from you and the closing exercises of our own Seminary year will probably prevent any of us from attending. We rejoice with you in the honored position of Dr. Green, and gladly recognize the debt of honor due him for his steadfast defence of the Word of God, and our prayer is that he may be long spared to you and to us all.

Yours very truly in Christ,

J. W. BEARDSLEE,
President of the Faculty.

RESOLUTIONS ADOPTED BY THE FACULTY OF XENIA THEOLOGICAL SEMINARY.

Whereas, The Faculty of Xenia Theological Seminary has been notified that a meeting will be held in Princeton, N. J., in celebration of the appointment of Dr. William Henry Green to be a Professor in the Seminary of that place, and has been, moreover, invited to be present on the occasion ; and

Whereas, It would be inconvenient for the Faculty as a whole, or for any of its members, to attend the proposed gathering ; and

Whereas, The Faculty is unwilling to appear indifferent in the matter ; therefore

Resolved, That the Faculty of the oldest Protestant Theological Seminary on this continent, with perhaps one exception (New Brunswick), learns with pleasure that Princeton Seminary proposes to honor Dr. Green on the occasion of the completion of his fiftieth year of service in that distinguished institution ;

Resolved, That as a Faculty we rejoice in the great work done by Dr. Green as an Instructor in the Seminary, as an educator through the medium of his unexcelled, if, indeed, not unequalled, Hebrew grammars, and as a writer in defence of the Word of God against subtle attacks made upon it in the name of scientific criticism, and we express the desire that for many years he may be spared to wield, as in the past, a powerful influence in behalf of genuine sacred learning and in vindication of the cause of truth.

Resolved, That the Faculty highly appreciates the honor done it in the invitation received, and hereby gratefully acknowledges the courtesy shown.

JAMES HARPER,
President.

CENTRE COLLEGE, KENTUCKY.

DANVILLE, KY., March 30, 1896.

MY DEAR SIR :

The Faculty of Centre College express through me their regret that Centre College cannot be present at the celebration of the fiftieth anniversary of the appointment of Professor William Henry Green as an Instructor in the Theological Seminary at Princeton, N. J., and express, also, their sincerest thanks to the Seminary for their kind invitation.

Hoping that the celebration will be delightful in every sense, I remain,
Very respectfully yours,

JNO. W. REDD,
Secretary of Faculty.

HAMILTON COLLEGE.

CLINTON, N. Y., March 23, 1896.

The Faculty of Hamilton College present their respectful congratulations to Princeton Theological Seminary upon the occasion of May 5th, and rejoice in the mature and historic usefulness of the careful and devout scholar, who is the Nestor of American Hebraists.

M. WOOLSEY STRYKER,
President.

SOUTHWESTERN PRESBYTERIAN UNIVERSITY.

CLARKESVILLE, TENN., April 6, 1896.

DEAR SIR:

Please express to your Committee my hearty thanks for the invitation to be present at the celebration of the fiftieth anniversary of Dr. Green's appointment as an Instructor in Princeton Seminary, and my regret that the special duties which will be upon me at that time will prevent my being present. I regret my inability to attend the more when I remember and rejoice that fifty years of Dr. Green's work is worth a hundred and fifty of most men's, and that God has set him here for the defence of the truth just at a time when such a man was most needed as a bulwark against the tide of destructive criticism which is arrogantly trying to sweep everything before it. May Dr. Green be given many more years to bless the Church and the world.

Yours truly,
GEORGE SUMMEY,
Chancellor and Professor of Biblical History.

PRESBYTERIAN COLLEGE, HALIFAX, NOVA SCOTIA.

PINE HILL, HALIFAX, N. S., April 2, 1896.

DEAR SIR:

On behalf of the Faculty of our College, I am instructed to say that we are grateful for the invitation to attend Dr. Green's Jubilee and that we much regret that we shall not be able to send a representative. None the less, however, do we wish every success to services held in honor of a name as much admired and revered in Canadian as in American churches.

Sincerely yours,
JOHN CURRIE,
Professor of Hebrew and Old Testament Exegesis in the Presbyterian College, Halifax, N. S.

KNOX COLLEGE, TORONTO, CANADA.

TORONTO, CAN., April 17, 1896.

TO THE THEOLOGICAL SEMINARY OF THE PRESBYTERIAN CHURCH IN THE UNITED STATES OF AMERICA, AT PRINCETON, N. J.

Dear Brethren: The Senate of Knox College returns thanks for your kind invitation to be represented at the celebration of the fiftieth anniversary of the appointment of Professor Green as an Instructor in the Seminary at Princeton. The Senate regrets that it cannot arrange to send one of its members to Princeton as its representative on so interesting an occasion, but it requests permission to express its high appreciation of the character and attainments of the distinguished teacher whose fiftieth year in the work of theological tuition is being commemorated and of the services which he has been honored to render to the Presbyterian Church and the Church Universal.

By his instructions as a professor and by his writings Dr. Green has proved himself one of the ablest and most successful defenders of the truth and authority of the Word of God ; and in an age when eminent theological scholarship has not seldom been found in union with defective views of divine truth, or has even led the way in depreciating the value of Scripture, Dr. Green's example has shown that the highest attainments in Biblical scholarship have no necessary connection with rationalistic tendencies. The Senate desires to unite with many in thanksgiving to God for bestowing upon His servant the eminent talents and the grace which have made him during his long course as a teacher a powerful and judicious defender of the true doctrine regarding the integrity and authority of the Inspired Word. We desire to assure Dr. Green of the esteem and honor with which he is regarded by the Senate and the Faculty of Knox College and of the Church under whose care the College is. We pray that he may be permitted to add not a few years of fruitful service to the fifty which are to-day commemorated, before he shall receive the "crown of righteousness" which the Lord shall give to those who "have kept the faith" and "have loved His appearing."

In the name of the Senate of Knox College.

Yours with highest esteem,
WILLIAM CAVEN.

PRESBYTERIAN COLLEGE, MONTREAL, CANADA.

MONTREAL, CAN., May 1, 1896.

MY DEAR SIR :

I am very sorry to be obliged to inform you that I find it now impossible to have the pleasure of being present at the Rev. Dr. Green's Jubilee celebration. Allow me at the same time to assure you that as a

College we enter most heartily into the spirit that has prompted the movement to do honor to this distinguished servant of God and the Church. In common with multitudes throughout Christendom we thankfully recognize the great things that have been accomplished for the cause of truth by his ripe scholarship and talented efforts. Our prayer is that God may yet more abundantly bless him and the Seminary with which he is connected.

Yours very truly,
D. H. MACVICAR,
Principal.

VICTORIA UNIVERSITY, TORONTO, CANADA.

QUEENS PARK, TORONTO, CAN.

The Faculty of Theology in Victoria University, Toronto, beg to acknowledge with thanks the kind invitation of the Theological Seminary of the Presbyterian Church in the United States of America at Princeton, N. J., to be present at the celebration of the fiftieth anniversary of the appointment of Professor Green as Instructor in that Seminary, to express regret that it will not be possible for any member of our Faculty to be present on that occasion, and to offer our sincere congratulations both to Princeton Seminary and to Professor Green on the completion of fifty years of such eminent service to the cause of theological learning and of the kingdom of our Lord Jesus Christ.

THE THEOLOGICAL COLLEGE OF THE PRESBYTERIAN CHURCH OF ENGLAND, LONDON.

THEOLOGICAL COLLEGE, LONDON, ENG.

REVEREND AND DEAR SIR :

I am honored by the invitation of the Theological Seminary that I should attend the Jubilee of Professor Green's connection with Princeton, to be held on May 5th. Unfortunately, the date is in any case an impossible one for me, as it falls too near the meeting of our Annual Synod, from which this year I could not well absent myself. But I am none the less grateful for the compliment which our sister College has paid to the institution over which I preside by addressing this friendly invitation to me. We are all of us proud to associate ourselves in spirit with the festivities by which Princeton is to celebrate the life-long services of one of her most distinguished teachers. The Senate of this College offers to

Professor Green through you, sir, its respectful congratulations, and for the famous Seminary which he has so long adorned we wish ever-increasing usefulness and fame as a seal of Presbyterian faith and sound scholarship.
Believe me to be, with cordial and fraternal salutations,
Yours most sincerely,
J. OSWALD DYKES,
Principal.

KINGS COLLEGE, LONDON.

KINGS COLLEGE, LONDON, ENG., March 2, 1896.

The Rev. Dr. Wace, Principal of Kings College, London, returns his hearty thanks for the invitation with which he has been honored to attend the celebration at Princeton, N. J., of the fiftieth anniversary of the appointment of the Rev. Professor William Henry Green, D.D. If it had been possible for Dr. Wace to be present, it would not only have given him the greatest pleasure, but he would have regarded it as a duty to avail himself of such an opportunity for testifying his gratitude to Dr. Green for the invaluable services he has rendered to the Church, especially during the last few years, in vindicating the truth of the Scriptures of the Old Testament. But the date of the celebration falls in the middle of the academical term in this College, when it is impossible for Dr. Wace to be so long absent from his official duties as would be required by a visit to America.

THE THEOLOGICAL FACULTY OF THE UNIVERSITY OF OXFORD.

CHRIST CHURCH, OXFORD, ENG., March 2, 1896.

DEAR SIR :

On behalf of the Theological Faculty of the University of Oxford, I have to acknowledge the receipt of an invitation to be present at Princeton on the occasion of the celebration of the fiftieth anniversary of Professor W. H. Green as a teacher in the Theological Seminary, but must express regret that none of us will be able to avail ourselves of it, as the date fixed, May 5th, falls in the very midst of our academical term, when our duties as professors and lecturers require our presence here.

I am yours faithfully,
WILLIAM INCE,
Regius Professor of Divinity, Oxford.

FREE CHURCH COLLEGE, ABERDEEN.

April 3, 1896.

DEAR SIR:

I have to acknowledge your courtesy in sending the letter of invitation to be present at the celebration of the fiftieth anniversary of the appointment of Professor William Henry Green as an Instructor in Princeton Theological Seminary. I regret to say that it is out of my power, as is the case, also, with my colleagues, to attend on the interesting occasion which is now in view. It would have been a peculiar pleasure to me to connect a visit to which I have long looked forward, but have not as yet accomplished, to the United States of America, with a celebration so remarkably deserved. As this cannot be, I desire, in my colleagues' name as well as my own, to express our high value for Professor Green's work and our satisfaction that it is to be recognized in this way. All who are interested in Old Testament studies, however they may differ in some things, will be as one in honoring Professor Green and in appreciating the important contributions he has made to scholarship. He is one from whom all can learn and whose fairness of mind all admire.

We rejoice very heartily in the honor done him, and we pray that the Seminary with which he has been so long connected may flourish largely in the future, as it has done in the past.

I am yours sincerely,
S. D. F. SALMOND.

THE FACULTY OF DIVINITY OF THE UNIVERSITY OF EDINBURGH.

UNIVERSITY OF EDINBURGH, April 23, 1896.

The Faculty of Divinity of the University of Edinburgh have delayed their reply to the invitation of the Theological Seminary, Princeton, N. J., in the hope that some one of the Faculty might be able to represent them at Princeton on May 5th next. They sincerely regret that there is now no prospect of this hope being fulfilled, but they appreciate none the less the consideration and cordiality which prompted the invitation. They fully reciprocate these sentiments, and tender their warm thanks to the Theological Seminary. They also offer their very respectful congratulations and best wishes to Professor Green, whose Jubilee the Seminary is about to celebrate.

M. C. TAYLOR,
Dean of the Faculty of Divinity.

NEW COLLEGE, EDINBURGH.

To Professor William Henry Green, D.D.

Dear and Honored Sir : In common with your many friends on both sides of the Atlantic, the professors in New College, Edinburgh, beg to congratulate you on the singular distinction of attaining your fiftieth anniversary as an Instructor in the Princeton Seminary of the Presbyterian Church in the United States of America.

Your long and successful labors have given you an almost unrivalled opportunity of influencing the large body of students for the ministry who have proceeded from your class-room. Your well-known works and numerous articles in the department of sacred literature, so assiduously cultivated by you, have extended your influence to a still larger circle of readers, both lay and clerical, and have done much to ripen questions of Old Testament scholarship. You have taken a large and honorable part in the discussion of these questions—a discussion in which your exact learning, devout spirit, and courtesy as a controversialist have been conspicuous.

This is not the first time we in Scotland have had the opportunity of honoring your name. We recall with satisfaction that our University here in Edinburgh, at its tercentenary, more than a decade ago, conferred upon you the well-merited distinction of its Doctorate in Divinity. Now that you have reached the rare term of half a century's labors as an instructor, we avail ourselves of this renewed occasion to express our sense of the valuable services you have been graciously spared to render to the Church of Christ throughout the world, and to join in the prayer that you may be long continued to extend these services.

We remain, dear sir, yours faithfully,
A. B. Davidson,
John Laidlaw.

Signed in our name and those of our colleagues:
Principal R. Rainy. D.D.,
Professor W. G. Blaikie, D.D.,
Professor John Duns, D.D.,
Professor Marcus Dods, D.D.

THE PRESBYTERIAN COLLEGE OF EDINBURGH.

Edinburgh, March 31, 1896.

The Principal and Professors of the United Presbyterian College, Edinburgh, desire to thank the Theological Seminary of the Presbyterian Church, United States of America, for their courtesy in inviting them to the celebration of the fiftieth anniversary of the appointment of Professor William Henry Green to office, but regret that none of them are able to be present on that most interesting occasion.

As a Senatus, however, they tender to Professor Green and to the Seminary of which he is so distinguished an ornament, their heartiest congratulations, and rejoice to unite thus in honoring one whose lifelong services in the cause of sacred learning are recognized in Britain no less cordially than in America.

J. A. PATTERSON, D.D.,
Clerk of Senatus.

THE THEOLOGICAL COLLEGE OF THE SCOTTISH EPISCOPAL CHURCH, EDINBURGH.

EDINBURGH, April 21, 1896.

The Theological College of the Scottish Episcopal Church is grateful for the kind invitation of the Princeton Presbyterian Seminary, and regrets that it has not been found possible to send a representative to the celebration on May 5th.

SCOTTISH CONGREGATIONAL THEOLOGICAL HALL, EDINBURGH.

EDINBURGH, April 6, 1896.

MY DEAR SIR :

The Committee of this Institution duly received your letter containing an invitation from the Theological Seminary of the Presbyterian Church in the United States of America, at Princeton, N. J., to be represented at the Jubilee celebration of the venerable Professor W. H. Green. While thanking your Committee for the honor of this invitation, I am instructed to express the regret of the Committee that circumstances prevent us from having the pleasure of accepting it. Trusting that the celebration will be, in all respects, most successful,

I remain, yours faithfully,
W. HOPE DAVISON.

FREE CHURCH COLLEGE, GLASGOW.

FREE CHURCH COLLEGE, GLASGOW, March 17, 1896.

TO THE THEOLOGICAL SEMINARY OF THE PRESBYTERIAN CHURCH IN THE UNITED STATES OF AMERICA, AT PRINCETON, N. J.

We, the Principal and Professors of the Glasgow College of the Free Church of Scotland, beg to acknowledge the kindness of the Theological

Seminary at Princeton in inviting our presence at the celebration of the fiftieth anniversary of the appointment of Professor William Henry Green as an Instructor in the Seminary on May 5th next. We are aware of the valuable contributions which Professor Green has made to the study and exposition of the Scriptures of the Old Testament ; and we desire to join in your congratulations and expression of thankfulness that he has been spared for the long period of fifty years to do fruitful service as a teacher in Princeton Seminary. We trust that he may still be enabled to continue these services and that he may have the blessing of God on himself and his work. We would also express our high esteem for Princeton Seminary and our sense of the good work which it has done and is doing for the cause of divine truth and the education of students for the ministry of the Gospel. We remember gratefully the help and encouragement which it gave to our Church in her contendings for the spirituality and freedom of the Church of Christ, and we pray for the Seminary, its teachers, and its students a continuance in the future of its honorable career of usefulness. One of our number, the Rev. George Adam Smith, D.D., Professor of Hebrew and Old Testament Exegesis in this College, expects to be in America at the time of the celebration, and, if consistent with his previously formed engagements, will have pleasure in attending and conveying to you the congratulations and good wishes in which we all cordially join.

In the name of the Principal and Professors :

JAMES S. CANDLISH,
Clerk of Senatus.

THE THEOLOGICAL FACULTY OF THE ALEXANDRIAN UNIVERSITY, AT HELSINGFORS, FINLAND.

HELSINGFORS, FINLAND, April 14, 1896.

REVEREND AND DEAR SIR :

The Theological Faculty of the Alexandrian University at Helsingfors feel very much obliged for the invitation received to be present at the solemn celebration of the fiftieth anniversary of the appointment of Professor William Henry Green as an Instructor in the Theological Seminary at Princeton, N. J., and return their most respectful thanks.

The Faculty, who would have felt themselves honored in taking part through a delegate in a celebration of so rare an occurrence, find themselves unable to do so, and are necessitated to present herewith their most respectful congratulations both to the aged Professor celebrating his Jubilee and to the Theological Seminary, which has been permitted to enjoy the great privilege during half a century to count among its teachers a man so highly respected for the scholarship and the intrepid courage that have characterized Professor William Henry Green.

Invoking the blessing of the Most High on him and on every labor connected with the Bible in the service of divine truth, we are, reverend and dear sir,
Yours very respectfully,

K. AUG. R. TÖTTERMAN, K. A. APPELBER,
S. EDR. STENIJ, G. G. ROSENQVIST,
O. F. COLLIANDER, E. JOHANSSON.

FACULTÉ DE THÉOLOGIE PROTESTANTE DE PARIS.

PARIS, le 10 Mars, 1896.
MONSIEUR ET HONORÉ COLLÉGUE :

La Faculté a recu l'invitation du Seminaire de Princeton à assister aux fêtes du jubilé des cinquante ans d'enseignement de M. le Professeur W. H. Green. N'oubliant pas qu'un de ses anciens membres, M. Edouard Reuss, a professé la Theologie pendant cent-vingt semestres, elle se réjouit de voir également une longue carrière d'enseignement accordée à un excellent collègue. Elle lui souhaite l'heureux continuation de son ministère et elle est heureuse de profiter de cette occasion pour exprimer aux professeurs de Princeton sa bien cordiale et fraternelle sympathie.

La Doyen de la Faculté :
A. SABATIER.

THEOLOGICAL FACULTY OF THE UNIVERSITY OF BERLIN.

BERLIN, den 9 März, 1896.
EW. HOCHWOHLGEBOREN :

Verdanken wir die freundliche Einladung zum Jubiläum des Professor Green bestens, und bedauern durch die Entfernung verhindert zu sein, uns an Ihrem Feste vertreten zu lassen.

Namens der theologischen Fakultät der Friedrich Wilhelm Universität zu Berlin :

SCHLATTER,
der z. Dekan.

THE EVANGELICAL THEOLOGICAL FACULTY OF BRESLAU.

BRESLAU, den 29 März, 1896.
DEM THEOLOGISCHEN SEMINAR DER PRESBYTERIANISCHEN KIRCHE ZU PRINCETON :

Beehre ich mich im Auftrag der evangelisch-theologischen Fakultät zu Breslau zu der bevorstehenden Jubelfeier unsre Glückwünsche zu senden.

Wir bedauern dass es keinem aus unsrer Mitte möglich ist, der freundlichen Einladung zur Theilnahme an Ihrer Festfeier Folge zu leisten. Dankbaren Sinnes gedenken auch wir der verdienstlichen Arbeiten des Jubilars D. D. H. W. Green auf dem Gebiete der hebräischen Grammatik und der alttestamentlichen Wissenschaft, und wünschen, dass seine und des ganzen theologischen Seminars Wirksamkeit reich gesegnet sein möge, der presbyterianischen Kirche theologisch fest gegründete und wohl ausgerüstete Diener am Wort heranzubilden.

In hochachtungsvoller Ergebenheit :
D. KAWERAU,
Prof. d. Theol., d. z. Dekan.

THE THEOLOGICAL FACULTY OF THE UNIVERSITY OF ERLANGEN.

ERLANGEN, den 5 März, 1896.

AN DAS THEOLOGISCHE SEMINAR ZU PRINCETON :

Die Einladung zur Theilnahme an der Feier des 50 jährigen Amtsjubiläums des Professors W. H. Green am 5 Mai a. c. hat die theologische Fakultät zu Erlangen als einen freundlichen Ausdruck der über den Ocean und über die Schranken der Confessionskirchen hinausreichenden Gemeinschaft christlicher und theologischer Überzeugungen dankbar in Empfang genommen und würde sich bei dieser seltenen Feier um so lieber persönlich vertreten sehen, als sie die ernsten Bemühungen des Herrn Jubilars um die Aufrechterhaltung der Würde des Alten Testaments wohl zu würdigen weiss. Der gütigen Einladung zu folgen ist uns jedoch, abgesehen von anderen Schwierigkeiten, schon dadurch verwehrt, das wir zur Zeit der beabsichtigten Feier durch unsere amtliche Verpflichtung verhindert sind, unsere Universitätsstadt für mehrere Wochen zu verlassen. Es bleibt uns daher nur übrig, dem theologischen Seminar und seinem hochverdienten Senior zu dem Jubiläum am 5 Mai unsere aufrichtigen Glückwünsche darzubringen und Gottes Segen zu wünschen.

In vorzüglicher Hochachtung,
D. TH. ZAHN,
d. z. Dekan der theologischen Fakultät zu Erlangen.

THE THEOLOGICAL FACULTY OF THE UNIVERSITY OF GIESSEN.

GIESSEN, den 30 März, 1896.

SEHR GEEHRTER HERR :

Ihrer Einladung zur Feier des fünfzigjährigen Jubiläums des Herrn Dr. William Henry Green am 5. Mai dieses Jahres vermag die Fakultät zu Giessen zu ihrem Bedauern nicht zu entsprechen. Die Fakultät hat jedoch

den unterzeichneten Dekan beauftragt, mit dem Danke für die Einladung Sie zu bitten, in ihrem Namen Herrn Dr. Green die herzlichsten Glückwünsche zu übermitteln und zugleich die hohe Schätzung zum Ausdruck zu bringen, die sie für die gelehrten Arbeiten des Herrn Jubilars hegt, Möchte Gott dem hochverdienten Manne noch manches Jahr weiteren Schaffens zulegen und möchte das Seminar von Princeton sich noch lange seiner Wirksamkeit in Segen erfreuen dürfen.
In vorzüglicher Hochachtung Ew. Hochwürden ergebener,
D. FERD. KATTENBUSCH,
Dekan der theologischen Fakultät.

THE THEOLOGICAL FACULTY OF THE UNIVERSITY OF GÖTTINGEN.

GÖTTINGEN, den 7 März, 1896.
GEEHRTER HERR :
Unsre Fakultät hat die freundliche Einladung zu Ihrem am 5ten Mai stattfindenden schönen Feste mit bestem Dank empfangen. Wenn ihre Mitglieder auch ausser Stande sind, Ihrer Aufforderung zu entsprechen, da zur Zeit Ihrer Feier unsre Arbeitszeit neu begonnen haben wird, so legen wir doch Wert darauf, Ihnen unsre Theilnahme an dem festlichen Tage und seiner Veranlassung auszudrücken, und bitten Sie, geehrter Herr, Ihren Herrn Collegen unsre besten Wünsche freundlich zu übermitteln.
In ausgezeichneter Hochachtung.
H. SCHULTZ, DR. TH.,
Dekan der theologischen Fakultät zu Göttingen.

THE THEOLOGICAL FACULTY OF THE UNIVERSITY OF GREIFSWALD.

GREIFSWALD, den 22 April, 1896.
EW. HOCHWÜRDEN :
Werden am 5ten des nächsten Monats den fünfzigsten Jahrestag Ihres Wirkens am Theologischen Seminar zu Princeton festlich begehen. Die Theologen Greifswalds schätzen sich glücklich Ihnen zu diesem Ehrentage ihre Glückwünsche darbringen zu dürfen. Sie thun dies, indem sie mit froher Theilnahme vor allem des reichen Segens gedenken, der während der verflossenen fünf Jahrzehnte unter Ihrer hervorragenden Mitwirkung von den Lehrstühlen Princeton's auf Nordamerika's evangelisch-theologische Jugend ausgegangen ist—eines Segens, von welchem während der letzten Jahre auch an unserer hiesigen Hochschule manches begeisterte Zeugnis aus dankbarem jugendlichen Munde abgelegt wurde. Und nicht minder preisen wir Gottes Gnade ob der Reihe trefflicher, vom Geiste

glaubensvoller Wissenschaft getragener Beiträge zur gelehrten Durchforschung der alttestamentlichen hl. Schrift, welche während des genannten Zeitraums von Ew. Hochwürden den theologischen Mitforschern wie in der neuen so in der alten Welt gespendet worden sind.

Wir bitten Gott den Herrn, er wolle Sie den bevorstehenden Gedenktag als einen Tag ungetrübter Freude inmitten Ihrer zahlreichen Schüler und Verehrer begehen lassen und Sie Ihrem so reich gesegneten Wirkungskreise noch viele Jahre in rüstiger Frische und Schaffenskraft erhalten.

Genehmigen Sie, hochgeehrter Herr College, die Versicherung der herzlichen und freudigen Theilnahme, womit wir, als im Geiste Ihnen nahe, Sie begrüssen und beglückwünschen.

Ew. Hochwürden verehrungsvoll ergebene
Theologische Fakultät der Univ. Greifswald :
DR. O. ZÖCKLER,
z. Dek.
Herrn Professor WILLIAM HENRY GREEN, D.D., LL.D.,
Princeton, N. J.

THE THEOLOGICAL FACULTY OF THE UNIVERSITY OF HALLE.

HALLE, A. S., den 9 April, 1896.
HOCHGEEHRTER HERR :

Am 2ten März a. c. ist die unterzeichnete theologische Fakultät mit einer Einladung zur Semisaecular-Feier des Herrn Professor Green am 5ten Mai dieses Jahres beehrt worden.

Wenn es uns nun auch unmöglich ist, uns an dem genannten Tage— zwei Wochen nach dem Beginn des Somersemesters—persönlich durch ein Mitglied der Fakultat vertreten zu lassen, so möchten wir es doch nicht an der Versicherung unseres warmen Anteils an diesem Feste fehlen lassen und richten daher an Ew. Hochwürden die ergebenste Bitte, dem hochverehrten Herrn Jubilar an seinem Ehrentage unsere herzlichen Glückund Segenswünsche übermitteln zu wollen.

Im Namen und Auftrag der theolog. Fakultät der Univers. Halle der Dekan,
D. E. KAUTZSCH.

THE THEOLOGICAL FACULTY OF THE UNIVERSITY OF JENA.

JENA, den 25 März, 1896.
HOCHGEEHRTER HERR :

Das theologische Seminar der Presbyterianischen Kirche in den Vereinigten Staaten von America zu Princeton, N. J., hat der theologischen

Fakultät zu Jena eine hohe Ehre erwiesen durch die gütige Einladung zu der Feier des 50 jährigen Amts-Jubiläums der Herrn Professor William Henry Green am 5 Mai d. Z. Alle Professoren unserer Fakultät beauftragen mich als den zeitigen Decan dem theologischen Seminar zu Princeton den herzlichsten Dank für diese Einladung auszudrücken. Wir müssen aber um freundliche Entschuldigung dafür bitten, das wir bei bestem Willen der gütigen Einladung nicht Folge leisten können. Am 5 Mai sind wir alle vollauf beschäftigt durch akademische Vorlesungen. Bei mir kommt noch hinzu, dass ich, so Gott will, am 25 Mai d. Z. selbst mein 50 jähriges Doctor-Jubiläum feiern werde. Es bleibt mir also nur übrig, dem würdigen Herrn Jubilar im Namen meiner Collegen die herzlichsten Glückwünsche zu der Vollendung eines halben Jahrhunderts in segenreicher Wirksamkeit auszudrücken. Gott gebe, dass er das schöne Fest noch lange in Gesundheit des Leibes und der Seele überleben möge.

Hochachtungsvoll und ergebenst,

Dr. A. Hitzenfeld,
d. z. Dekan der theol. Fakultät.

THE THEOLOGICAL FACULTY OF THE UNIVERSITY OF KÖNIGSBERG.

Viro summe reverendo pientissimo doctissimo
GUILELMO HENRICO GREEN
in Seminario Theologico quod Princetonii floret Professori
Hebraistarum Americanorum Nestori venerabilissimo
de studiis Hebraicae Grammatices trans Oceanum promovendis optime
merito
collegii virorum Angloamericanam librorum Veteris Testamenti versionem
ad textus originalis amussim emendare jussorum praesidi
Moysis et Pentateuchi contra criticorum sententias defensori acri strenuo
impigro qui
Deo Trino favente
propediem muneris sacra semisaecularia feliciter acturus est
hunc ipsum solemnem atque laetum diem
ex intimo corde congratulatur
ordo Theologorum in Universitate Albertina docentium
Datum Regiomonti Prussorum anno post natum Redemptorem nostrum
MDCCCLXXXXVI die VIII ante Kalendas Maias
Cornill
h. a. decanus.

THE THEOLOGICAL FACULTY OF THE UNIVERSITY OF LEIPZIG.

LEIPZIG, Anfang April, 1896.

HOCHGEEHRTE HERREN COLLEGEN:

Sie haben die Güte gehabt uns mitzutheilen, dass Herr Professor William Henry Green, in Princeton, New Jersey, am 5ten Mai d. J. sein 50 jähriges Amtsjubiläum begeht, und auch uns dazu eingeladen.

Wir danken aufrichtig für die Einladung und nehmen an Ihrer Ehren-Feier aufrichtigen Anteil. Leider verbieten uns die Entfernung und amtlich die Zeitlage des Semesters der Einladung persönlich Folge zu leisten. Aber wir begrüssen mit unseren Segenswünschen gleichfalls die seltene Jubelfeier eines Lebens, welches durch rastlose Thätigkeit und gründliche Gelehrsamkeit in einen Umkreis alttestamentlicher Arbeiten eingegriffen hat, die grade in den letzten Jahrzehnten und noch fortgehend die Wissenschaft und Kirche auf das Tiefste bewegen, und nur allmälig geklärt und ausgetragen werden können. Jede gediegene Mitarbeit ist hier mit Dank zu begrüssen. Auch wir bringen diesen Dank und diese Anerkennung dem Herrn Jubilar und den evangelischen Brüdern Nordamerikas, und bitten diese Gesinnung auch unsererseits am Jubeltage selbst zum Ausdrucke bringen zu wollen.

Möge der Herr noch manches Jahr dem verehrten Manne und dadurch auch der Wissenschaft schenken, der er mit treuem Gewissen und sorgfältigem Forschen sein Leben hindurch hat dienen wollen.

Mit den Grüssen collegialischer Verehrung und Ergebenheit.

Die theologische Fakultät:

DR. G. A. FRICKE,
d. z. Dekan der theol. Fakultät.

THE THEOLOGICAL FACULTY OF THE UNIVERSITY OF MARBURG.

MARBURG, den 11 März, 1896.

Für die sehr gefällige Einladung auf den 5ten Mai d. J. zur Feier des Jahrestages der Ernennung des Professor William Henry Green als Lehrer an dem Seminar zu Princeton vor fünfzig Jahren sagen wir dem Theologischen Seminar unseren verbindlichen Dank. Zu unserem Bedauern ist Keiner von uns im Stande, an der Feier persönlich Theil zu nehmen. Wir sprechen aber zu derselben unsere herzlichsten Glückwünsche aus im freudigen Bewusstsein der vielfachen Wechselbeziehungen, die zwischen dem Theologischen Studium in Amerika und bei uns bestehen. Wir erinnern uns gerne der jungen Theologen aus Amerika, die auch unsere Fakultät von Zeit zu Zeit besucht haben. Wir hoffen, dass zu unserer beiderseitigen Förderung in christlicher Gemeinschaft und in theologischer Arbeit die freundlichen Beziehungen zwischen Ihrer theologischen Schule und der unsrigen dauernd fortbestehen werden.

GRAF BAUDISSIN,
d. z. Dekan.

An The Theological Seminary of the Presbyterian Church in the United States of America, at Princeton, N. J.

THE THEOLOGICAL FACULTY OF THE UNIVERSITY OF MUNICH

Send their best respects and congratulations to the Theological Seminary of the Presbyterian Church in the United States of America, at Princeton, N. J., on account of the celebration of the fiftieth anniversary of the appointment of Professor William Henry Green as an Instructor in the Seminary. By

PROFESSOR DR. T. BACH,
The present Dean.

March 15, 1896.

THE THEOLOGICAL FACULTY OF THE UNIVERSITY OF STRASSBURG.

STRASSBURG (ELSASS), den 29 März, 1896.

DEM THEOLOGISCHEN SEMINAR DER PRESBYTERIANISCHEN KIRCHE ZU PRINCETON :

Sagt der Unterzeichnete Namens seiner Fakultät den verbindlichsten Dank für die gütige Einladung, die ihr zu Teil geworden, und verbindet damit die herzlichsten Grüsse und Glückwünsche fur die Anstalt und ihre Lehrkräfte. Mögen diese dürftigen Zeilen weil sie aus der Stadt Bucers und Calvins kommen in Ihren Augen einen Werth gewinnen, den ihnen unsre Namen zu geben ausser Stande sind.

Der Dekan der theologischen Fakultät an der Kaiser Wilhelms-Universität.

D. JULIUS SMEND,
p. p. o.

THE EVANGELICAL FACULTY OF THE UNIVERSITY OF TÜBINGEN.

TUBINGEN, den 9 April, 1896.

Dem theologischen Seminar zu Princeton, New Jersey, sendet die evangelisch-theologische Fakultät der Universität Tübingen zu seiner 50 jährigen Jubelfeier die aufrichtigsten Glück-und Segenswünsche.
Im Namen der Fakultät der derzeitige Dekan derselben :

PAUL BUDER,
Professor Dr. Theol.

THE THEOLOGICAL FACULTY OF THE UNIVERSITY OF GRONINGEN, HOLLAND.

GRONINGEN, March 10, 1896.

The Theological Faculty of the University of Groningen is, to its regret, prevented from accepting the courteous invitation of the Theological Seminary of the Presbyterian Church in the United States of America, at Princeton, N. J.

C. H. DeRHYN,
Secretary.

THE THEOLOGICAL FACULTY OF THE UNIVERSITY OF LEIDEN.

LEIDEN, March 15, 1896.

The Theological Faculty of the University of Leiden regret to be prevented from sending a representative at the celebration of the fiftieth anniversary of the appointment of Professor William Henry Green as an Instructor in the Seminary of the Presbyterian Church in the United States of America, at Princeton, N. J.

W. N. KOSTERS,
Secretary of the Theological Faculty.

THE THEOLOGICAL FACULTY OF THE UNIVERSITY OF UTRECHT.

UTRECHT, March 6, 1896.

DEAR SIR :

The Theological Faculty of the University of Utrecht regret the impossibility of assisting at the Jubilee of Professor William Henry Green. The Faculty feel much honored by your kind invitation and send you

their sincere congratulations on the privilege of having Professor Green so long a time as an Instructor in your Seminary. The Faculty also beg you to express their congratulations to Professor Green himself.
Respectfully yours,
T. H. VALETON,
President of the Faculty.

THE THEOLOGICAL FACULTY OF THE UNIVERSITY OF NORWAY.

KRISTIANIA, NORGE, March 26, 1896.

DEAR SIR :

On behalf of the Theological Faculty of the University of Norway, I feel obliged to return our deep-felt and most respectful thanks for your highly valued and esteemed invitation to the Jubilee of Professor Green, and regret very much that the Faculty, on account of work and the long voyage, cannot have the pleasure of accepting the invitation. We beg you kindly to give our most respectful compliments to Professor Green, and we pray that the blessings of our Heavenly Father may rest upon him, and that he may be spared yet longer for his blessed work for the Church.
Yours in Christ sincerely,
DR. SIGURD ODLAND,
Professor Theologiæ.

THE THEOLOGICAL FACULTY OF THE UNIVERSITY OF COIMBRA, PORTUGAL.

COIMBRA, 13 de Março de 1896.

A Faculdade de Theologia da Universidade de Coimbra muito agradece o vosso amavel convite. A longo distancia que separa esta Universidade do Seminario theologico da egreja presbyteriana dos Estados Unidos e o serviço das aulas, que não pode ser interrompido, são motivos poderosos que obstam a que a Faculdade de Theologia possa ser representada nas festas com que o vosso Seminario vae celebrar o quinquagesimo anniversario da nomeação do professor William Henry Geeen.
DR. LUIZ MARIA DA SILVA RAMOS,
Decano da Faculdade de Theologia.

THE CATHOLIC THEOLOGICAL FACULTY OF BERN, SWITZERLAND.

BERN, den 13 März, 1896.

Sie hatten, geehrter Herr, die Güte, unserer Fakultät eine Einladung des Theologischen Seminars zu Princeton zur Feier des fünfzigjährigen Jubiläums des Herrn Professors W. H. Green zu übersenden. Zu unserm Bedauern verbietet uns die weite Entfernung durch persönliche Abordnung eines unserer Mitglieder uns an dieser Feier zu beteiligen. Empfangen Sie daher auf diesem Wege die Glückwünsche unserer Fakultät zu einem so seltenen Feste für den ehrwürdigen Gefeierter und für das Seminar.

Mögen die Arbeiten Ihrer Anstalt auch fernerhin von reichem Gottessegen begleitet sein! Genehmigen Sie, geehrter Herr, die Versicherung unserer ausgezeichneten Hochachtung!

Die Katholisch-theologische Fakultät der Hochschule Bern.

DR. ADOLPH THÜRLINGS,
Dekan.

THE THEOLOGICAL FACULTY OF THE UNIVERSITY OF GENEVA.

GENÈVE, le 2 avril, 1896.

MONSIEUR :

C'est avec un vif regret que je dois vous annoncer qu'aucun professeur de notre Faculté ne pourra se rendre à Princeton pour la fête qui sera donnée en l'honneur de Monsieur le professeur William Henry Green. Mais nous serons avec lui de cœur et de prière ce jour-là, et nous vous remercions chaleureusement de l'invitation que vous avez eu l'aimable attention de nous adresser et que la *distance* nous empêche d'accepter.

Votre respectueusement devoué,

J. M. COUGNARD,
Doyen.

THE THEOLOGICAL FACULTY OF THE UNIVERSITY OF LAUSANNE.

LAUSANNE, le 30 avril, 1896.

MONSIEUR ET HONORÉ FRÈRE EN JÉSUS-CHRIST :

Il est bien tard pour venir, au nom de la faculté de théologie de l'Université de Lausanne, vous remercier cordialement de l'invitation que vous nous avez adressé, il y a quelques semaines, pour participer au jubilé cinquantenaire de l'enseigment de monsieur le professeur William Henry Green au séminaire théologique de Princeton. Professeurs d'une faculté de théologie se rattachant à une Eglise presbytérienne comme la vôtre, nous eussions aimé pouvoir apporter en personne nos félicitations et nos vœux à l'éminent professeur dont vous fêtez le jubilé, et profiter de cette occasion pour lier, avec les professeurs de votre illustre faculté de théologie, des rapports personnels. Vous comprendrez facilement, monsieur, en présence de la grande distance qui nous sépare, l'impossibilité où nous sommes de réaliser ce desir, et vous excuserez par consequent aisément notre absence à Princeton le cinq mai.

Par contre nous tenons à vous assurer qu'en ce jour-là nous serons de cœur et d'esprit avec vous. Avec vous, nous rendrons grace à Dieu pour les longs et loyaux services qui a rendus à votre Eglise M. le professeur Green dans l'étude de la Bible et spécialment de l'Ancien Testament. Avec vous, nous demanderons à Dieu de lui conserver aussi longtemps que possible force spirituelle et physique pour continuer sa tâche. En vous priant, monsieur et honoré frère, de bien vouloir transmettre au jubilaire l'expression de nos felicitations et de nos meilleurs soutraits, je tiens à ajouter que notre faculté fait les meilleurs vœux pour la prosperité du seminaire théologique de Princeton. Puisse-t-il, pendant de longues années, fournir à l'Eglise de Jesus-Christ, des hommes sachant unir l'amour de la vérité à la chaleur de la piété.

C'est dans ces sentiments de cordial intérêt pour votre faculté et votre Eglise et de chrétienne affection pour ses professeurs et ses étudiants, que je vous prie, monsieur et honoré frère, d'agréer l'expression de mes sentiments fraternels.

Au nom de la faculté de théologie le doyen :

LOUIS EMERY.

THE THEOLOGICAL FACULTY OF THE UNIVERSITY OF ZÜRICH.

ZÜRICH, den 13 März, 1896.

AN HERRN WILLIAM HENRY GREEN, D.D.

Hochgeehrter Herr : Zu der seltenen Feier der fünfzigjährigen Amtsthätigkeit als theologischer Dozent, die Sie, hochgeehrter Herr, am 5ten Mai dieses Jahres begehen, bringen wir Ihnen unsere herzlichen Glückwünsche dar.

Es ist Ihnen vergönnt gewesen, während der langen Zeit von 5 Jahrzehnten Ihre Krafte in den Dienst des Reiches Gottes zu stellen und zu seiner Ehre zu wirken. Sie haben durchdrungen von dem hohen Ernst der Wissenschaft und der Verantwortlichkeit, die jedem akademischen Lehrer, vor mella aber den Vertretern der theologischen Wissenschaft auferlegt ist, mit hingebenster Gewissenhaftigkeit und Treue, mit tief eindringender Gelehrsamkeit und Sachkenntniss selbst nach dem gerungen was Wahrheit ist, und Sie haben auch die wissenschaftlichen Arbeiten und Bestrebungen Anderer mit Scharfsinn und milder Objectivität geprüft, ihre Wahrheitsmomente gern und freudig anerkannt und gegenüber abweichenden Anschauungen die eigene Überzeugung mit edelm Ernste geltend gemacht. Im solchem Geiste haben Sie mit unablässigem Eifer die europäische Wissenschaft nach der neuen Welt verpflanzen helfen und haben in Ihren Schülern den Grund gelegt, der sie zu selbständigen wissenschaftlichen Streben und zu gründlicher eigener Forschung befähigte. Alles diess hat Ihnen überall da, wo wissenschaftlicher Forschungseifer, Treue in der Berufsthätigkeit und charactervolles Eintreten für die eigene Überzeugung etwas gelten, Achtung und Verehrung erworben, und insbesondere die Mitarbeiter der theologischen Wissenschaft schulden Ihnen, auch wenn sie mit den Ausgangspuncten oder den Ergebnissen Ihrer Forscherthätigkeit nicht übereinstimmen, den wärmsten Dank und die grösste Anerkennung für den hohen Ernst Ihrer Arbeit.

Um des Segens willen, in solcher Weise wirken zu können, und um des Segens willen der von dieser Wirksamkeit ausgegangen ist, wofür wir mit Ihnen Gott die Ehre geben, beglückwünscht Sie, hochverehrter Herr College,

Die theologische Fakultät der Universität Zürich (Schweiz).
In deren namen,
PROF. VON SCHULTHESS RECHBERG,
Der Dekan.

THE THEOLOGICAL FACULTY OF THE UNIVERSITY OF UPSALA, SWEDEN.

DEAR SIR:

The Theological Faculty at Upsala have with great pleasure received your invitation to send a member of the Faculty to assist at the celebration of the illustrious Professor Green's anniversary, but we deplore the impossibility of being able to accept your kind and honorable request on account of our present session, which continues till the end of May, and during which time all of us are strictly at work.

Yours most respectfully,
PROFESSOR CARL MORRBY, D.D.,
Decanus.

LETTERS OF REGRET FROM INDIVIDUALS.

Rev. William Alexander, D.D., Professor in San Francisco Theological Seminary.

I regret exceedingly that it will be impossible for me to be present with you in honoring Dr. Green. No one is more deserving of honor than he is. Fifty years of continuous service, and especially such service as he has rendered, is of rare occurrence. Although there have been several others who are good seconds, yet Dr. Green has for a number of years been *facile princeps* in his own department. With ample learning and scholarship of the first rank, he has for years stood forth as the Coryphæus of orthodoxy in defence of the integrity of the Bible against the assaults of the destructive rationalistic criticism. I count it among the fortunate incidents of my life to have sat at the feet of such a man, and as I cannot be present, I gladly contribute my mite in this way. Please to assure Dr. Green of my continued love and veneration.

Rev. Wm. M. Blackburn, D.D., LL.D., President of Pierre University.

In expressing thanks for the invitation to attend the celebration in honor of Dr. W. H. Green and my regrets that I shall not be able to be present, permit me to say that one of my very strong convictions as a student in his classes, from 1851 to 1854, was that he was especially " set for the defence " of the Old Testament literature ; and from that time to the present I have had such confidence in his judgment on all questions concerning it that I have rested in his decisions. While his scholarship and instructions have extended over still broader ground, his greatest work thus far seems to have been in making more clear to this age the historical foundations of all Biblical literature, and consequently of faith in divine revelation through Sacred Scripture. This work is worthy of recognition by the celebration proposed.

Rev. S. F. Breckinridge, D.D., Professor of Exegetical Theology in the Theological Seminary of Wittenberg College, Springfield, O.

The invitation of the Theological Seminary of the Presbyterian Church in the United States of America, Princeton, N. J., to be present at the celebration of the fiftieth anniversary of the appointment of Professor William Henry Green as an Instructor in the Seminary has come to my hand. Although I have not the honor of a personal acquaintance with Professor Green, I have used for so many years his thorough-going and practical text-books of the Hebrew language and literature, and, I may add, with so much satisfaction and efficiency, in the class-room, that I sometimes imagine that I am well acquainted with him. At all events, the service which he has done for the Church at large by the preparation of these books, by his scholarly defence of the Bible as the Word of God, by his trenchant criticism of unfounded assumption, and the telling exposure of the plausible fallacies of its assailants, as well as by his eminent services in the lecture-room, he has won the lasting regard and gratitude of all the friends of the Church of our Redeemer. Pressing engagements will prevent my being present at the festive occasion to which I have been so kindly invited. Please convey to this honored servant of God assurances of my personal esteem and of my appreciation of his invaluable service to the cause of sound scholarship and orthodox Christianity.

Rev. G. Stockton Burroughs, D.D., President of Wabash College.

MY DEAR DR. GREEN:

I appreciate very highly the honor of being selected to say a few words, as a pupil of yours, on the occasion of the celebration of the fiftieth anniversary of the commencement of your work in connection with Princeton Seminary. It was with profound regret and a sense of personal loss that I found it impossible to be present, and was obliged to so write Dr. Warfield. It would have been a great privilege to have striven to give to others some share in the pleasing and profitable memories of the time spent in your class-room under your instruction. Nor are my memories confined to the class-room. It is the general impression which you made upon me, as scholar and man, out of the class-room as well as in it, that has been of especial benefit. I recall your conference talks on Sabbath afternoons, your sermons, the helpful personal interviews, characterized by kindly interest and wise counsel, as combining with your instruction to make my stay in the Seminary worth so much then and its influence since so helpful. It was, I believe, the background of these things which made the instruction so potent for good. You will permit me to thus send you my personal congratulations and the expression of my high regard and hearty thanks for personal benefits. You cannot know all that you have done for the large number whom you have touched with the influence of your life, but I am sure that the little which can be expressed to you will enable you to join with your many pupils in gratitude to our Heavenly Father for His especial kindness to you, and through you to them and the cause of Christian learning.

Rev. Edward L. Curtis, D.D., Professor of Hebrew Language and Literature in Yale University Divinity School.

Allow me to present my thanks for the invitation to be present at the celebration of the fiftieth anniversary of the appointment of Professor William Henry Green as an Instructor in the Princeton Seminary and my regrets that I am unable to accept it. While I have never had the privilege of the personal instruction of Professor Green, I take pleasure in acknowledging an indebtedness to him, which all Old Testament students must feel. In America, if not in the world, he is *facile princeps* in expounding and defending the sacred Scriptures of the old covenant upon the lines of the traditional views of the Christian Church, and however much some of us may feel, in certain particulars, compelled to differ with him in opinion, it is a delight to honor one who in solid learning, judicial fairness, and Christian courtesy has been surpassed by none in these days of controversy over the nature of the Bible.

Rev. George E. Day, D.D., Dean of the Theological Faculty of Yale University.

I cannot promise to myself the pleasure of being present at the celebration in honor of my esteemed friend, Professor Green, but beg you to convey to him personally the assurance of my interest in the proposed expression of appreciation of his work in the Seminary, the revision of the English version of the Old Testament, and his various contributions to Hebrew learning and literature.

Rev. Francis B. Denio, D.D., Professor of Old Testament Language and Literature in Bangor Theological Seminary.

PROFESSOR W. H. GREEN, D.D.

Reverend and Respected Sir: Permit me to congratulate you on your completion of half a century of service in the work of giving instruction in sacred literature in the Seminary which you have served and honored. I congratulate you on the fruitfulness of these years of service, both through your pupils and through the medium of the press. I wish, also, to express my thankfulness that you have been able to publish so much which has been of use in correcting extreme views gendered by crude progress in the development of Biblical knowledge and in forcing scholars to pause and reconsider conclusions which at times were too hastily adopted. With the hope that much more of fruit may come to us, and with the heartiest wishes for your continued health and strength, I remain. . . .

Rev. Timothy Dwight, D.D., LL.D., President of Yale University.

MY DEAR PROFESSOR GREEN :

I beg you will allow me to express to you my most sincere and hearty congratulations on the occasion of your fiftieth anniversary as a teacher and professor. It would give me very great pleasure to be present at the commemoration ceremonies, and to offer you these congratulations in person, but it now seems impracticable for me to do so. Professor Fisher will, at our request, represent our University and our Divinity School. He will bear to you our kindliest greeting and the testimony of our great respect and esteem. Let me, for myself personally, assure you of my best wishes for the future years of your working, which I trust may be many. You have the greatest reason for joy and satisfaction in your review of the past. Your life's work has not only been a most honorable and useful one, when viewed in itself, but it has been multiplied in its results and influences beyond measure, and it has moved into the lives and working of the large company of those who in these many years have received your instructions and the inspiration of your mind and spirit. Your pupils everywhere will bear you on their hearts at this happy season, and will offer their most earnest prayers that the peace of God may be with you. I am happy to have had the privilege of knowing you in the pleasant relations of the companies who met so often in the work of the revision of the English version of the Bible. I am happy at this time to unite with the survivors of those companies in a greeting of friendship for one whom we have so long honored as a friend and one who has done so much for the honor of American scholarship. Kindly give these few words of mine a place among the many congratulatory words which you are receiving in this jubilee year, and be assured that they are written in the sincere hope that the benediction of the divine Father may rest upon you now and always.

Rev. Owen H. Gates, Ph.D., Professor of Old Testament Language and Literature in Oberlin Theological Seminary.

The invitation courteously extended to me to be present at the celebration of the fiftieth anniversary of the appointment of Professor Green upon the Faculty of your Seminary I am obliged to decline, because of the imperative nature of my duties here at that time. I beg to congratulate the Seminary and Professor Green as well, upon his long service, and to express my appreciation of the extraordinary qualities of person and scholarship which have made the long connection with you possible and profitable. We are to be congratulated in view of Professor Green's notable contributions to Old Testament scholarship.

Rev. James Gibson, D.D., Edinburgh, Scotland.

I much regret my inability to accept the courteous invitation of the Princeton Theological Seminary to the approaching celebration of Dr. Green's Jubilee. In honoring him the Seminary honors itself. It is indeed something for any institution of sacred learning to boast of—or rather to give thanks for—that it has so long possessed such a distinguished champion of the truth. On my side of the Atlantic as well as yours Dr. Green's writings are held in the highest respect, even by those who have been swept off their feet—let us hope only for a time—by the turbid inrush of Dutch and German criticism. Let us hope and pray that Dr. Green may long be spared to lift up a standard against it, and to train up faithful men who will be able to meet learning with greater learning, and to contend both earnestly and successfully for the integrity and trustworthiness of the Inspired Word. . . .

Rev. Edward J. Hamilton, D.D., Professor of Mental and Moral Philosophy in Washington State University.

Nothing could be more agreeable to my feelings than to be present on May 5th, if my circumstances had not rendered it impossible. The graduates of Princeton Seminary are very widely scattered over our country and the world. Those of us who are on this distant side of the continent must, for the most part, content ourselves with sending you our fond recollections and our kindest wishes. Professor Green is the only remaining member of that noble Faculty whose instructions I enjoyed forty years ago. The memory of him, as he then was, in the first full maturity of his powers—modest, dignified, serious, earnest, laborious, and thorough; skilful to instruct, eloquent in preaching, thoughtful and considerate of others, and ever showing a tender and reverential piety—yet dwells with me, and exerts now, as it has already done, an uplifting and ennobling influence. I honor Professor Green greatly as a scholar and a teacher and as a most able advocate of truth, but I am still more impressed with the power of his stainless Christian life; and when I think how many during these last fifty years have received like benefits with me from the labors and the example of the good man, I thank God, who has so blessed his servant with long-continued usefulness. . . .

Rev. Henry M. Harman, D.D., LL.D., Professor of Greek and Hebrew in Dickinson College.

PROFESSOR WILLIAM HENRY GREEN, D.D., LL.D.

My Dear Doctor: I heartily congratulate you upon the fiftieth anniversary of your connection with Princeton Theological Seminary, whose fame you have done so much to maintain and augment. You have rendered splendid and most valuable service, not only to the Presbyterian Church, but to the Christian world. Your most excellent Hebrew Grammar and your writings in defence of the Pentateuch put you in the first rank of the Biblical scholars of the world. May God grant you many more years of usefulness. I greatly regret that my ill health prevents me from the journey to Princeton to join in rendering honor to one who well deserves the honors of the Christian world.

Rev. Charles C. Hersman, D.D., LL.D., Professor of Biblical Literature in Union Theological Seminary, Virginia.

As one of Dr. Green's pupils, now a large body extending over the whole Church, I unite with others to do him reverence. His profound and varied scholarship has given lustre to our American seminaries, his able defence of the truth has endeared him to all evangelical Christians who hold fast the old landmarks, and his keen Damascus blade has pierced the joints of the enemies' harness. The fifty years that have passed since he entered upon his work have been marked by wonderful revelations in the department of Biblical study and criticism. He has not only kept abreast of the highest advancement, but has himself been a leader. In its permanent results his work has been second to none, at home or abroad, not even to that of his great co-laborer, Dr. Charles Hodge. What the one has done for theology the other has done for Biblical study, the mother of theology. These two servants of God have rendered Princeton illustrious among the schools of the prophets. The name of William Henry Green is imperishably linked with the honored dead and the honored living, who have stood for the Word of God as given in Moses and the Prophets. May his bow long abide in strength and his mantle, when he departs, fall on some of his pupils who shall follow the venerable and beloved teacher in his spirit and aim.

Rev. Moses D. Hoge, D.D., of Richmond, Va.

DEAR DR. GREEN:

Among the letters of love and congratulation you are receiving on the completion of fifty years of service in the Princeton Theological Seminary please accept another, coming from one who cherishes a profound regard for you personally and for the memorable work you have accomplished. When Dr. Chalmers resigned his pastoral charge to become the teacher of those who were to be the future pastors of the Church, he felt that he was taking his position at the fountain-head of influence instead of spending all of his days beside one of the streams. Such has been the wisdom of your course under the guidance of divine Providence ; and the instruction you have given to such a multitude of candidates for the ministerial office, without relinquishing your own privilege as a preacher of the Gospel of our Lord as often as the opportunity offered, and the contributions you have made through the press in defence of our most holy faith have given you a place in the confidence and gratitude of your brethren due to the oldest of our theological professors. I hope it will not seem presumptuous in the humble pastor of a single church for fifty years to add my tribute of thankful recognition of what you have achieved in the wider and nobler field of your labors, and to express the hope that the God whom you have served so long and well, may crown the years that remain to you with a usefulness even surpassing what has already been attained.

Rev. Samuel M. Hopkins, D.D., Emeritus Professor in Auburn Theological Seminary.

I accept with entire content my natural sentence of old age and infirmity, but I regret that it should absolutely forbid my attending on the very interesting occasion of the fiftieth anniversary of the appointment of Professor William Henry Green as Instructor in the Theological Seminary. I had flattered myself that at the time of my retiring from the Chair of Church History in Auburn Theological Seminary, two years ago, I was the oldest living professor in any such school, having begun my term of service in the year 1847. But I believe that Princeton will bear away the palm for having enjoyed not merely one, but the two most "antiquated" professors in this or almost any other country. The labors of Dr. Green for half a century have shed a lustre on American sacred scholarship which will not be seriously dimmed by any difference of opinion as to the value of this school of criticism in which he is easily head master. The industry, the patience, the courage displayed in the championship of sound science for so long a time, claim the admiration of all scholars. It is no small praise in such a service to stand even as an *Athanasius contra mundum.* Wishing the highest success to so notable a celebration, so honorable alike to the Seminary and to the distinguished Professor, . . .

Rev. Herrick Johnson, D.D., LL.D., Professor in McCormick Theological Seminary.

DEAR DR. GREEN :
I cannot allow the occasion of your fiftieth anniversary as an Instructor in Princeton to pass without letting both my judgment and my heart speak in admiring and grateful recognition of your distinguished service. I congratulate the Seminary on, and thank God for, this half-century of

instruction. You have made it noble and beautiful with your ever-ripening scholarship and your ever-deepening convictions. It stands as an enduring monument of reverent learning and devotion. It is proof, too, that high culture and prolonged and profound study are consistent with a sweet reasonableness and a heart open and sympathetic to all real progress. I recall the days of the Committee on Revision of our Confession, when we came into unusually close and precious fellowship, and I remember with grateful appreciation the catholicity of your spirit and the broadness of your sympathy, and the valuable contributions they furnished to our fraternal conferences and doctrinal discussions. May God give you years yet of useful and honorable service.

Rev. John M. King, D.D., Professor of Old Testament Interpretation in Manitoba College, Winnipeg, Canada.

I desire to acknowledge with thanks the courtesy of the invitation addressed to me to be present at the celebration of the fiftieth anniversary of Professor Green's appointment as an Instructor in Princeton Seminary. I regret it will not be in my power to be present, not only because of the great distance, but also because I shall be engaged at the date of the celebration in the active work of our summer session in theology. I am glad, however, to have this opportunity for expressing my high regard for Professor Green and my sense of the important service which he has rendered during these fifty years to the cause of learning by his scholarly and yet cautious, reverent work in Old Testament inquiries, and I would wish to be permitted to join in this way in the tribute of esteem which is being appropriately paid to him.

Rev. Joseph J. Lampe, D.D., Professor of Old Testament Literature and Exegesis in Omaha Theological Seminary.

DEAR DR. GREEN:

The invitation to attend your fiftieth anniversary has been on my table for some days. It would give me much pleasure to attend and congratulate you personally, but the distance makes it impossible. Dr. Harsha will represent our Faculty on the occasion. I have never been privileged to attend your instruction in the class-room, but have often been helped by your books and published articles. Most heartily do I congratulate you on all that the Lord has enabled you to accomplish. Your services have been and are now of great value to the cause of Christ, and my prayer is that the Lord may keep you yet many years in your field of useful labor.

Right Rev. A. N. Littlejohn, D.D., LL.D., Protestant Episcopal Bishop of Long Island.

Public duties on May 5th will prevent my attending the celebration of the fiftieth anniversary of Professor Green's appointment as Instructor in the Theological Seminary at Princeton. I am glad to know that Professor Green is to be suitably honored at the end of a half century of most distinguished service in the field of Christian learning and theological instruction. His personal character, great attainments, and fruitful labors, to say nothing of what he has done to extend over the whole land the name and influence of the Institution with which he has been so long connected, richly deserve all that can be said and done to give dignity and emphasis to the proposed celebration.

Rev. Matthew B. Lowrie, D.D., Professor in Omaha Theological Seminary.

MY DEAR DR. GREEN :

It would have been impossible for a boy to have grown up in my father's household without acquiring for yourself a sincere respect and admiration. Your friendship for my father was the means of directing my steps to Princeton College, and my own acquaintance with you formed while there was what took me to Princeton Seminary. How much of my whole life has been decided by these early influences it is not hard to trace. You have surely under God been a marked element of Providence to me, and for this I am sincerely thankful. I also recognize the fact that what I have personally received from you is only a very small part of the good you have done by your life and teachings, and I count it a high privilege to unite with the great number of grateful pupils and friends, as we come back to express our gratitude and love to you, and praise God that your life has been spared to continue so long in far-reaching and deeply important and valuable service for the Church of God. With hearty congratulations upon the occasion of this anniversary, and the prayer that for many years to come we may continue to enjoy the benefit of your presence with us and your invaluable labors in the cause of truth, . . .

Rev. A. J. Maas, S. J., Professor of Sacred Scriptures and Hebrew in Woodstock College.

The kind invitation to Professor William Henry Green's fiftieth anniversary as Instructor in Princeton Seminary reached this place during my absence ; the delay of answer has therefore been unavoidable. Owing to a previous engagement, I cannot accept the invitation for Tuesday, May 5th. I regret this the more on account of my great admiration for the Professor's personal merits and the conservative character of his works. May Providence bless him with many more years of literary and scientific usefulness.

Rev. R. G. MacBeth, of Winnipeg, Canada.

I am just in receipt of the invitation to the Jubilee celebration of Dr. Green's appointment as an Instructor in the Seminary. As I go East in June to the General Assembly in Toronto, I regret that I cannot go to Princeton in May. But in the most entirely heartfelt manner I can say that I shall be with you in spirit and with the distinguished company that will assemble there to pay every tribute of honor and love to the great and good man upon whose life and work God has so unmistakably set the seal of His approval. A long letter from me on such an occasion would be uncalled for and even presumptuous, but as one who has been called upon to take some humble share in the development of this greater West of Canada, in which I was born, I would like to acknowledge my deep indebtedness to Dr. Green for precept and example, inculcating an unquestioning faith in God and God's Word and impressing upon those who met him in class-room, or library, or elsewhere, a noble ideal of Christian manhood.

Rev. W. J. McGlothlin, Instructor in Hebrew and Old Testament in the Southern Baptist Theological Seminary.

In acknowledging the receipt of the invitation with which you have honored me I am compelled to express my regret that pressing duties in the Seminary will not permit of my presence at the celebration of the anniversary. The great denomination to which Dr. Green belongs has honored itself in thus honoring this learned and godly man who has so long been its servant. Through you I hope to present the congratulations of one among the many who have not seen his face, but who have sat at his feet. I here record my devout thankfulness to Almighty God for the gift of this learned and devout scholar, this distinguished teacher, and earnest defender of the faith. May many years yet crown his head with usefulness and honor.

Rev. John Macmillan, M.A., of Belfast, Ireland.

I beg to thank you for the kind invitation to be present at the forthcoming Jubilee of Dr. Green. I am exceedingly sorry that circumstances do not permit my acceptance of it. However, as far as my sympathies with the promoters of the celebration, my affectionate regard for the Seminary, and my admiration and cordial good wishes for the venerated Professor are concerned, I can sincerely declare that on Tuesday, May 5th, "There shall be no more sea." I shall be with you in spirit, picturing the scene, living in the light of other days, and awaiting with much interest the published report of the proceedings. In common with all his students whom I have met since 1878, I feel profoundly grateful to Dr. Green for his influence in the class-room, which was not merely intellectual to a high degree, but also deeply moral and spiritual. His voice and manner have kept following me with the message, " Life is real, life is earnest." We are all proud of his unique position as a scholar and defender of the sacred oracles. His name—*clarum et venerabile nomen*—is equally respected on both sides of the Atlantic, and his books are almost as eagerly looked for by the ministers of our Church as of yours. Respect for his attainments and character is not confined to any school of thought or criticism ; it is universal. His last book, which I read a month ago, and which is so fresh, vigorous, and satisfactory, recalls to one's mind the description of the man whose delight is in the law of the Lord : " He shall be like a tree planted by the rivers of water that bringeth forth his fruit in his seasons ; his leaf also shall not wither ; and whatsoever he doeth shall prosper."

Rev. Dunlop Moore, D.D., of Pittsburg, Pa.

Dr. Green is pre-eminently worthy to be congratulated and honored at the completion of that long stadium of most laborious and valuable service. I take pleasure in testifying my personal indebtedness to him for aiding me to maintain my faith in the Scriptures of the Old Testament against the attacks of the destructive critics. The Church at large has cause to thank God for what He has enabled him to do in defence of divine truth in this age of aggressive and widespread unbelief. I do not think that I should, as so many in these last days have done, have abandoned all confidence in the Old Testament as a supernatural revelation, even if I had not studied the writings of Professor Green. But it would be extremely ungrateful on my part not to acknowledge the blessing that they have been to me. I have counted it a duty to bear witness repeatedly in public to the exceeding value of Dr. Green's contributions to the apologetic literature of the Old Testament. As late as yesterday, in writing to a distinguished theological professor in Scotland, I endeavored to induce him to use his influence in bringing Dr. Green's last and, as I think, greatest work (" The Unity of Genesis ") to the attention of that large number of Scotch ministers who have become more or less the victims of the negative critics. My earnest prayer is that the Lord may long preserve Dr. Green to serve the cause to which he has devoted his life.

Rev. William E. Moore, D.D., LL.D., of Columbus, O., Permanent Clerk of the Presbyterian General Assembly.

I have the invitation of the Theological Seminary of the Presbyterian Church, U. S. A., to be present at the celebration, May 5th, of the fiftieth anniversary of the appointment of Professor William H. Green as an Instructor in the Seminary. It would give me great pleasure were it in my power to comply with the invitation, and in person to unite with his many friends in congratulating both him and the Seminary on what God has done through him in these fifty years of his faithful service for our own Church and the Church at large. It was not my privilege to sit as a pupil at the feet of Dr. Green, but I have, I trust, profited by his labors through the press. I count it among the highest privileges and honors of my life to have been officially associated with him in the public affairs of the Church, and so to know the man and to love him as a Christian brother as well as to admire him as a Christian scholar. I am glad that Princeton gives to our common Presbyterianism and to our common Christianity the occasion in this celebration for calling to grateful remembrance the many services to the Church and to his humble brethren of our genial, modest, sincere, and earnest Christian scholar and teacher. May God spare him to you and to us for yet many years of fruitful labor and rich enjoyment. Please convey to him my sincere regard for him and my grateful appreciation of his friendship.

Rev. Walter W. Moore, D.D., LL.D., Professor of the Hebrew Language and Literature in Union Theological Seminary, Virginia.

Please accept my thanks for your courteous invitation to be present at the celebration of the fiftieth anniversary of the appointment of Professor William Henry Green as an Instructor in the Theological Seminary at Princeton. It is a matter of profound regret to me that urgent business with the Board of Directors of our own Institution, which cannot be delegated or postponed, will require my presence here on the very day which you have named as the date of the celebration. I am, therefore, constrained, although with extreme reluctance, to deny myself the pleasure of witnessing the exercises of this notable occasion. But I desire to express through you my cordial congratulations to Professor Green and the Seminary upon the completion of fifty years of faithful and fruitful service. Thoughtful and evangelical men the world over render unfeigned thanks to Almighty God as they contemplate the long and illustrious career of the venerated scholar whose Jubilee you thus commemorate. And well they may. For during these years he has moulded hundreds of ministers of the Gospel who have become pastors after God's own heart, feeding the people with knowledge and understanding. In addition to the benefit which successive classes for half a century have received from his oral instructions, he has enriched the literature of his department by various contributions of lasting value. To say nothing of the strong and full flow of his review articles, continued from year to year, and touching every subject—philological, exegetical, and critical—that has interest for the thorough-going student of the Old Testament, I can myself recall eight volumes that he has published since 1861, not counting his monumental grammar of the Hebrew language, and he "still brings forth fruit in old age." The estimation of his ability and general scholarship by those who have had the best opportunity of knowing him was shown nearly thirty years ago by his election to the Presidency of the College of New Jersey, which, on being declined by Dr. Green, was tendered to Dr. McCosh. The estimation of his character and learning by other scholars in the same department may be inferred from his selection as Chairman of the American Old Testament Company of the Anglo-American Bible Revision Committee. To-day he is pre-eminent among American Hebraists and Biblical critics of every shade of theological opinion. He is the revered and trusted leader of the younger conservative scholars in every branch of the Church. He is the foeman accounted most worthy of their steel by those who belong to the more radical schools of contemporary criticism. It must be accounted a special mark of God's favor to your Seminary and the Church, that during these years which have witnessed the fiercest conflict between the adherents of the old views and the advocates of the new the chair of Old Testament Literature in our most largely attended Presbyterian Seminary has been occupied by a man whose talents, learning, and discretion have been equalled only by his faith, his courage, and his zeal for truth. May the good hand of God be upon him as the shadows lengthen on his path, and in the grateful retrospect of honorable work faithfully accomplished may his heart be filled with a peace and cheer like those of the aged apostle, which shall be to him pledges of that still more precious reward which awaits all faithful followers of our Lord Jesus Christ. May his life be long spared to the Seminary and the Church for which he has labored so assiduously and successfully, and the distinguishing favor of the Most High continue to rest upon your venerable institution in all its influence and work.

Rev. Edward D. Morris, D.D., LL.D., Professor of Systematic Theology in Lane Theological Seminary.

Hardly anything I can think of in that line would give me as great pleasure as to be present as a witness of the commemorative exercises in honor of the long and eminent services of Dr. Green. For many years I have known him by reputation as among the ablest and wisest exegetes in our Church or in the country. But since I had the privilege of being closely associated with him in the Committee on the Revision of our Standards I have honored him in my thought and loved him with all my heart in a degree unknown before. I look back on that period of intimate fellowship with increasing pleasure as the years go by; and I would be glad to take some humble place in the assemblage of pupils and friends gathered to pay him the honors so justly his due. Our anniversary occurs on that very day; and I hope on that day to be saying my own *nunc dimittis* after nearly thirty years of service in this less conspicuous sphere. His long day of labor, like mine, is drawing to its close. At evening-time may there be abundant light on his faith; so prays his sincere friend.

Rev. J. B. Mowat, D.D., Professor of Hebrew, Chaldee, and Old Testament Exegesis in Queen's University, Kingston, Canada.

I thank you very much for the invitation to attend the semi-centennial celebration in honor of Professor Green. Circumstances will prevent my attendance upon that very interesting occasion, but I doubt if among those who will be present any one feels a higher admiration and reverence for Dr. Green than myself. As the chair which I have occupied for the last thirty-nine years in Queen's University—Hebrew, Chaldee, and Old Testament Exegesis—is similar to his, I have had a good opportunity of knowing how much the Church is indebted to him for the learning and ability which have spread his name and fame far beyond Princeton and his own land. He is a tower of strength to us of the old school. When we are taunted with a preponderance of experts who have adopted the new views of the Bible it is a great comfort and satisfaction that we can point to Dr. Green as one who has no superior among English-speaking higher critics for scholarship, and yet holds as firmly as ever that our blessed Lord was an infallible teacher and that every scripture is inspired of God. I hope Dr. Green will be spared for years after his fiftieth anniversary has come and gone to do more of such work as he has already done in behalf of Biblical science.

Rev. Frederick A. Muhlenburg, D.D., LL.D., of Reading, Pa.

. . . Though having always been a member of the Lutheran Church, I was a student in Princeton Theological Seminary during the winter term of 1838, and have kept in kindly remembrance the able Christian soldiers whose valuable instructions I there enjoyed. The wise and venerable Dr. Archibald Alexander; the learned, methodical, and polite Dr. Samuel Miller; the mild and logical Dr. Hodge, the eloquent and enthusiastic Dr. Breckenridge; and in Hebrew, that wonderful scholar and genius, Professor Joseph Addison Alexander, made an indelible impression on my memory and heart. My knowledge, love, and continued study of the Hebrew language to this year were the result of his tuition and inspiration. One of my genial classmates, with a fond affection common to us all, used to call him "the literary curiosity." What bright luminaries to teach others! *Quid veritas et quid sapientia possit.* It is my misfortune not to have a personal acquaintance with Dr. Green, but I have often been edified and instructed by his judicious and learned explanations of the Old Testament, in opposition to the so-called "higher criticism," and have made use of his Hebrew Grammar. Thus I can say he is a worthy successor of those who have preceded him in the long line of illustrious teachers. May God grant him many more years of usefulness in his honorable office and a happy reunion with those who have gone before him to the better land.

Rev. Joseph Packard, D.D., Professor of Hebrew and Biblical Learning in the Theological Seminary of the Diocese of Virginia.

It would give me great pleasure to be present at the semi-centennial anniversary of Dr. Green's professorship, but my age and infirmity will compel me to decline your invitation. I have always regarded Dr. Green as without a superior in Biblical learning. The whole Church honors him as a defender of the faith against the assault of the higher criticism. As a member of the Old Testament Company of the Revision of the Authorized Version, I can testify to his valuable services as president of the company.

Rev. James Park, D.D., of Knoxville, Tenn.

An unusually protracted absence from home has hindered a more prompt reply to the invitation, and but for this my answer would have been a glad acceptance instead of regrets of my inability to attend. Since I first heard of the intended celebration of this anniversary it was my desire to be present on the occasion, but a serious indisposition, which necessitated an absence of some weeks from my charge, has also put it beyond my ability to go to Princeton. But my heart will be with you in according to Dr. Green all the honor due for his long and faithful service, and in the grateful acknowledgment of God's goodness and grace in continuing his efficient labors through all the fifty years by which so much honor and glory have been brought to the good name of Princeton and the Presbyterian Church. My recollection of him as a fellow-student, whom we loved for his diligence, fidelity, and conscientious discharge of duty, as well as for his genial companionship, is pleasant and vivid, although so many years have passed away. May the blessing of our covenant-keeping God abide with Dr. Green and Princeton Theological Seminary always.

Rev. William L. Pearson, Ph.D., Professor of Biblical Literature and Exegesis in Penn College, Oskaloosa, Ia.

Please accept my heartiest thanks for yourself and all the friends of Professor William Henry Green who have honored me with an invitation to the celebration of the fiftieth anniversary of his appointment as Professor in Princeton Theological Seminary. It is with great regret that I find it impracticable to be present on an occasion of so much interest to a very large number of friends and students of Dr. Green. It was my good fortune to pursue my studies after I was graduated from the Seminary under the direction of Professor Green and to be otherwise pleasantly connected with him. If distance and duty did not prevent it, I should deem it a great privilege to be present at this very important anniversary. This is an event not for Princeton students alone, nor for Presbyterians alone ; all Protestantism should find satisfaction in the half century's work of such a Biblical scholar. In the providence of God Dr. Green's professional labors began about the time the negative criticism had fairly come into prominence, and it has probably had no abler opponent nor a worthier one. This is substantially the opinion expressed by the late W. Robertson Smith in a letter to a professor of theology in Berlin soon after "Moses and the Prophets" appeared. His students will always remember and reverence Dr. Green most for his deep piety, his love of truth, and his untiring devotion to their daily instruction. But they have been truly gratified to observe their distinguished teacher standing for years firmly with the few, and later on, though almost alone, yet highly respected even by his opponents, as the defender of the genuineness and entire trustworthiness of the Bible, a tower of strength unshaken, though often assailed. And it is their great pleasure to believe that his influence will increase in years to come with the progress and growing moderation of Biblical criticism. It is needless to assure you of the admiration and love of a truly attached student of Dr. Green.

Rev. J. N. Rendall, D.D., President of Lincoln University.

I find that I must forego the honor and the pleasure of being present at the celebration of the fiftieth anniversary of Dr. William Henry Green's professional appointment at the headquarters of our American Presbyterianism. The Theological Faculty of Lincoln University have sent a delegation, and a number of my colleagues will be personally present. In honoring Dr. Green all Presbyterians honor the Church for whose Biblical foundation and historic constitution Princeton Theological Seminary has from its origin contended, as for "the faith once delivered to the saints." The Alumni of Princeton Theological Seminary have great reason to take part in the joy of this celebration. Dr. Green represents the whole life of the Seminary. He was the pupil, the associate, and the friend of the eminent men who laid the foundation of its greatness. He was one with them in their reverence for the Word of God as the infallible rule of faith and duty. He was one with them in their appreciation of the indispensable importance of a broad and thorough scholarship, both for the defence of the truth, and for the preservation of soundness in doctrine in the Church itself. And he is like them in presenting himself an example of the union of the most profound research in the whole field of evidence and interpretation, together with the most liberal charity toward all who cannot lightly speak evil of our Lord Jesus Christ, even though they follow not with us. Dr. Green's influence has always been helpful to the spirituality of the students of the Seminary, stimulating to their scholarship, and expanding to their Christian sympathies. And the welcome which, whether present or absent, we all give to this anniversary, means our hope and confidence that the union of sound learning and sound theology exemplified in his life may never be separated in Princeton. But his reward is the approbation of the Lord, and not our praise.

Rev. Matthew B. Riddle, D.D., LL.D., Professor in the Western Theological Seminary, Allegheny, Pa.

MY DEAR DR. GREEN :

Our Faculty will, we trust, be represented at your approaching Jubilee as a teacher in theology, and give formal expression to our congratulations. I cannot, however, deny myself the gratification of addressing you personally in view of this auspicious occasion. Though we have not been associated in special lines of study, it happens that you and I are the only persons who were members of three Committees on Revision, that of the English Bible, of the Westminster Confession, and of the Proof Texts appended thereto. It happens, moreover, that coincident with your own Jubilee will be the completion of twenty-five years of continuous service on my part in the department of New Testament Exegesis. Except Dr. Morris, of Lane, who has resigned, though still in service, you are the only professor in any theological seminary who was occupying a chair when I began in 1871. It is hard to believe that in seniority of service I stand next to yourself, but it seems to be true. Dr. Beecher, of Auburn, began when I did, but all the others are our juniors. This state of things warrants me in sending you a special note of congratulation.

Rev. Robert W. Rogers, D.D., Professor of Hebrew and Old Testament Exegesis in Drew Theological Seminary, Madison, N. J.

. . . The day when William Henry Green began to teach at Princeton is a day now historic in the annals of Oriental study in America. We who are essaying to do teaching and to carry on research in this department are nearly all his sons, even if we have never enjoyed his personal instruction. It is well to pause in order to commemorate so great a day and to honor so noble a scholar. I could join heartily in it if I were so happy as to be able to be present.

Rev. Charles A. Salmond, M.A., of Edinburgh, Scotland.

It would give me the greatest pleasure to revisit the *alma mater*, especially on so interesting an occasion as the celebration of Professor Green's Jubilee. But, alas! three thousand miles of ocean lie between, so that I cannot possibly be with you then. Accept my warmest thanks none the less for the invitation, and be assured that I shall be present in sympathy, if not in bodily appearance, at the celebration. Dr. Green is one whom the great brotherhood of the Seminary Alumni may well delight to honor. When we think of the successive bands of students who have been impressed not only with his powerful intellect and his rare scholarship, but by his lofty Christian character and his gracious Christian bearing, who will venture to measure the influence he has exerted directly and indirectly during these fifty years? Dr. Green is the only member now alive of the Seminary Faculty as I remember it in 1877 and 1878. To me he is enshrined in heart as well as in memory with Charles and Alexander Hodge, as a noble example of consecrated Christian manhood, loyally and unflinchingly devoted to the service of the truth, like them. He is held in reverence by many on this side as well as on your side of the Atlantic, for, like them, he belongs to all the Churches. To Dr. Green himself as well as to all assembled on May 5th, it will be a great element of joy to note the continued prosperity of the Seminary, and to know that the Princeton tradition is still in the hands of a body of teachers so worthy to be the successors even of the remarkable men who have gone before them.

Rev. Thomas J. Sawyer, D.D., Professor Emeritus in Tuft's Divinity School.

I thank you cordially for the kind invitation to be present at the coming celebration of the fiftieth anniversary of the appointment of Rev. Dr. Green as Instructor in the Princeton Theological Seminary. The occasion will be honorable to the man and the institution. I have long been acquainted with the Doctor's learning, labors, and character, and nothing would give me greater pleasure than to share with his numerous friends and former pupils in doing him honor. But my age—being now in my ninety-third year—the distance, and the fatigue incident to the undertaking all unite to admonish me that prudence is the better part of valor, and that safe at home and in my own neighborhood I must content myself with reading, or rather having read, the account of what my eyes are forbidden to see and my ears originally to hear. I shall, I am sure, be present with you in spirit on May 5th, and thus witness with pleasure the honor paid to sound learning and the unity of the Christian religion, in which I, with you and all sincere believers, rejoice.

Rev. George H. Schodde, Ph.D., Professor of Greek and Hebrew in the Lutheran Theological Seminary at Columbus, O.

I have received from your Committee an invitation to attend the anniversary celebration of Dr. Green on the fifth of next month. While deeply regretting the fact that I cannot be personally present, I cannot deny myself the pleasure of congratulating both the institution and Dr. Green on this occasion. There is no theologian in America whom I delight more to honor than Dr. Green, whose extraordinary work in defence of old Bible truth has endeared him to our Church, that counted among its own sons the original Henstenberg, whose spirit and scholarship Dr. Green so well represents in our own day. It is my hope and prayer that the honored Old Testament veteran of Princeton may continue for many years yet to defend the truth as he has done in the past.

Rev. George Adam Smith, D.D., Professor in the Free Church College, Glasgow.

REVEREND AND DEAR SIR:

The Faculty to which I belong—the Divinity Professors of the Free Church College, Glasgow—had the honor of an invitation to the celebration of your Jubilee as a professor. We sent answer that, if I found it compatible with my other engagements, I would count it an honor and pleasure to be present. Unfortunately it is not in my power to be in Princeton on Tuesday to assist in doing honor to one to whom all Old Testament scholars look up as a scholar and critic. I beg, therefore, to be excused, but I hope to visit Princeton later on, when I shall probably have better opportunities of meeting you and of making your acquaintance than if I were to come on Tuesday. Besides the personal tribute which I would have brought to yourself, sir, I would have come charged with the expression of gratitude and cordial esteem toward Princeton, whose help and encouragement, shown so richly to the Free Church of Scotland at the time of her foundation, is not forgotten by us, and never shall be.

APPENDIX

Rev. Richard S. Storrs, D.D., LL.D., of Brooklyn, N. Y.

I feel it an honor, as it certainly is to me a great pleasure, to present through you my most hearty congratulations to Dr. William H. Green and to the Theological Seminary at Princeton on the completion of fifty years of his most honorable and useful connection with that distinguished institution. I have hoped to be able to do this personally in attendance upon the proposed services to-morrow ; but as this is made impossible by the urgency of other imperative calls upon me, you will, I hope, do it by these few written words. Dr. Green and his work have been known to me for many years, and no Christian scholar has been more highly honored by me. The work of no one has commended itself to me as more careful and thorough, more rich in best elements of power, more instructive and animating to the minds of students, more fully pervaded by the spirit of appreciative independence of human guides, of intelligent and profound reverence toward God and His Word. His have been the great privilege and the great responsibility of teaching teachers in all this half century of years ; and the influence which through them has gone so widely over the country has been always one of the streams which make glad the city of God. It has been an influence for thoughtful and serious study, for reverential faith in the divine " Book for the world," for surer trust in its majestic and tender promises, for larger and more eager effort to extend the knowledge of it to all mankind. He has stood self-poised and assured amid the whirls of changeful and conflicting opinions, and the assaults of a scepticism, avowed or insidious, have been met by him with a commanding composure and a fulness of refutation which have given strength to the weak and courage to the timid while exalting his praise among the most eminent scholars of the time. Surely he is to be congratulated on the great work which the Master has thus permitted and aided him to accomplish ; the Seminary is to be congratulated on having so long enjoyed his most faithful and fruitful services; and we all, of whatever communion, may congratulate ourselves on the beauty and the power which he, " without haste and without rest," has imparted to our faith and to our ministry.

Rev. Milton S. Terry, S.T.D., Professor of Old Testament Exegesis and Biblical Theology in Garrett Biblical Institute, Evanston, Ill.

I sincerely regret that it will be impracticable for me to be present at the celebration of the fiftieth anniversary of Professor Green's appointment as Instructor at Princeton. The entire Evangelical Church, I doubt not, is more than ready to congratulate him in the good providence which has enabled him to fill out such a monumental record. I desire to bear my personal testimony to the inspiration and help which Professor Green's published works have been to me for twenty-five years in my studies in Hebrew and Old Testament exegesis, and also to express my profound respect for his ability, his scholarship, and his fidelity to the truths of divine revelation.

Rev. Cornelius Van Santvoord, D.D., of Kingston, N. Y.

I have received your kind invitation to be present at the celebration of Professor Green's semi-centennial, and had intended to acknowledge it at once, and trust you will pardon my remissness in not doing so. It will give me great pleasure to revisit Princeton after an absence from it of many years, and to contribute, however slightly, to show honor to one whom the whole Church honors as well for the great services he has done it all these years as for his high character as a religious teacher and Christian man. I recall with lively sensibility the days when, more than half a century ago, I enjoyed the instructions of the Alexanders, father and son, and of Drs. Miller, Hodge, and Breckinridge, whose influence upon my own humble life and labors I have never failed to acknowledge and feel grateful for. The most of those with whom I associated as students have, with the teachers, been gathered to the fathers since then, and we who remain must follow them ere long ; and while we do remain, I am sure there is not one whose heart does not go out toward Princeton Seminary in grateful recognition of the good received from it and in earnest good wishes and prayers for its abiding prosperity.

Rev. D. M. Welton, D.D., Professor of Hebrew and Old Testament in McMaster University, Toronto, Canada.

In reply to your favor recently received, in which you do me the honor to ask me to be present at the celebration of the fiftieth anniversary of the appointment of Professor William Henry Green as an Instructor in the Princeton Seminary, I have to say that I very deeply regret that, owing to the closing exercises of McMaster University occurring at the same time, in which I am expected to take some part, it will not be possible for me to share in the high privilege and honor which your very courteous invitation has put before me. In giving expression, however, to this regret, I beg to say, also, that if there is any man in the world whose writings have been of special value to me, any man to whom the whole Christian world is greatly indebted for his masterly defence of Biblical and Christian truth, any man whom I profoundly esteem and delight to honor, that man is Dr. William Henry Green, of Princeton. My earnest prayer is that his years and strength may be greatly multiplied, so that long yet he may continue to serve the Master in his chosen field of inquiry.

Rev. W. G. Williams, LL.D., Professor of Biblical Literature, etc., in the Ohio Wesleyan University.

I return most hearty thanks to the Theological Seminary at Princeton for the invitation to the fiftieth anniversary of Professor Green's appointment as an Instructor in the Seminary. I should most gladly be present with you upon that occasion, but it comes at a date when I shall find it impossible to be absent from college duties. But I most cordially sympathize with you in this appropriate recognition of the long services of the distinguished man whom you and all the world delight to honor. Professor Green's admirable work is known in all the land and his praise is in all the Churches. We know him and honor him as a great teacher, as an author, as a defender of the faith, and as a man of exemplary life and character; and thousands to-day greet him from afar in the name of the common Church of Christ and of the cause of Christian education. One who has also been a teacher here, in one position, for more than fifty years, sends his heartiest congratulations to Professor Green, and prays that yet many years may be added to his useful and honored life.

Rev. John L. Withrow, D.D., of Chicago, Ill.

I will not be able to attend the celebration exercises, May 5th, in honor of the beloved Senior Professor of the Theological Seminary; but it is with much more than ordinary emotions of regret that this announcement is made. Dr. William Henry Green did more for me than any teacher in my student days. I have ever since revered him more than any living man. It may not appear so to all, but to me it seems as if he has served to steady the forces of truth-seekers on theological lines as no other scholar of the century has. Has there ever been a fair refutation of his reasoning in support of the traditional belief in the Bible as the very Word of God?

Rev. Charles H. H. Wright, D.D., Grinfield Lecturer on the Septuagint in the University of Oxford, England.

I received yesterday (just before starting to deliver a lecture at Cambridge) the kind invitation to attend the Jubilee of Professor W. H. Green, D.D., on May 5th. I regret that I cannot attend your Jubilee, as the expense would be too great, but I cordially greet the learned Professor on the coming Jubilee. His works have been of inestimable importance in the past, and will prove even more important in the future. I most heartily greet him as one of the very best representatives of the conservative school of Old Testament criticism, a school of critics which, I believe, will yet win the day.

Rev. Dr. Adolph Zahn, of Stuttgart, and Rev. Edward Rupprecht, of Sausenhofen, Germany.

HOCHGEEHRTER HERR PROFESSOR.

Hochwürdiger Herr: Bei Ihren fünfzigjährigen Amtsjubiläum nahen Ihnen auch zwei deutsche Theologen, um Ihnen ihren warmen Dank auszusprechen für die vielfache Belehrung und Anregung, die sie in Ihren ausgezeichneten Schriften gefunden haben.

In Deutschland von aller guten Apologetik für die heiligen Bücher des A. T. verlassen, inmitten einer trostlosen Negation und Verwirrung, die bis zur völligen Ableugnung aller göttlichen Offenbarung im A. T. sich steigerte, und die mit dem bekannten Stolze der deutschen Gelehrten vorgetragen wurde, mit der in unserem Vaterlande bei jedem neuen Fundlein wiederkehrenden anmassungsvollen Behauptung dass man es mit "sicheren Ergebnissen der Wissenschaft" zu thun habe, trat uns in Ihnen dem Chief of staff of the Army of American Hebrew and Old Testament students eine Leitung und Unterstützung entgegen, die uns mit den besten Mitteln der Gelehrsamkeit, des klaren Verstandes, der scharfsinnigen Einsichtung, vor allem der tiefen Pietät gegen Gottes Wort die vortrefflichsten Dienste leistete. In unserer Einsamkeit entdeckten wir Sie jenseits der grossen Wasser und freuten uns über das helle Licht, das uns aus der Ferne entgegenleuchtete. Wir wurden in unserer Verlassenheit durch Sie ermütigt und gestärkt, auch für Deutschland wieder den Kampf für die Wahrhaftigkeit und Zuverlässigkeit des A. T. aufzunehmen und allen Behauptungen des kindischen Wahnes tapfer entgegenzutreten. Was wir nicht wussten, wussten Sie, und wir schöpften reichlich aus Ihren immer klaren, ruhigen und unwiderleglichen Gedanken.

Wir kennen unser gelehrtes Deutschland. Man fühlt sich bei uns wohl wenn man alles immer wieder mit einen Mitteln bekritteln und verneinen kann; der Eifer ist anfänglich Himmelhoch, der Zulauf—namentlich der Jugend bedeutend, mit allen Posaunen wird geschmettert, das man nun endlich hinter das Geheimnis des A. T. gekommen sei—aber das hält in Deutschland nur eine gewisse Zeit an; man steigert sich in eine masslose Verwirrung hinein, man kauft die Bücher dann wird man müde, man bekommt Überdruss an seiner Geschäftigkeit—und man bricht ab, was man aufgebaut. Nachdem man Kirchen des Inlandes und Auslandes vergiftet hat, nachdem man die Grundlage der Reformation zerstört hat, erklärt man mit kalter Ruhe, das sich diese Hypothesen nicht halten lassen. So hat der Protestantismus in Deutschland sein Spiel getrieben seit Mitte des vorigen Jahrhunderts und wird es weiter treiben, wenn Gott ihm noch eine Scheinleben lässt.

Wir wollen es doch heute vor der gesamten amerikanischen Welt, in der ein Bibel noch so viel gilt, gerade an Ihrem Ehrentage, hochwürdiger Herr, zur Befestigung mancher aussprechen; der Pseudoprotestantismus hat in Deutschland bei unausgesetzter kritischer Arbeit auch keine einzige Thatsache, kein einziges Ergebniss ermittelt, ja er hat nicht einmal die bessere Erkentniss der menschlichen Entstehung der heiligen Schriften gefördert. Wohl Ihnen, hochwürdiger Herr, dass Sie den deutschen Einfällen nicht geglaubt, sondern ihnen festen Wiederstand geleistet haben und so auch uns gestärkt haben. In den herrlichen Räumen des berühmten Princeton, in mitten vieler wackerer Schüler, wohlbekannt jenseits und diesseits des Oceans feiern Sie in ehrwürdigem Alter nach Mühe und Fleiss ein ehrenreiches Jubiläum. Das ist doch der grösste Ruhm, der Ihnen zufällt ; Sie haben überall der Schrift mehr geglaubt als den Ansichten irrtumsvoller Menschen. Mit den herzlichsten und aufrichtigsten Glück-und Segenswünchen gesellen auch wir uns unter die Freunde, die Ihnen Heil zurufen ! Möge die Barmherzigkeit Gottes noch lange erhalten und Sie in allem guten Werke fördern.

Ihre ergebenen Dr. th. and lic. th.

ADOLPH ZAHN,
reformirter Pfarrer in Stuttgart.
EDUARD RUPPRECHT,
Pfarrer in Sausenhofen in Bayern.

PRESS ARTICLES.

The Presbyterian Banner of April 15, 1896.

. . . As Chairman of the American Company for the Revision of the Old Testament, Dr. Green occupied a most conspicuous and responsible place, which he filled with great ability and in a way most highly creditable to American scholarship. In 1891 he was Moderator of the General Assembly which met in Detroit, and discharged the duties of his position most acceptably. He was also a member of the Second General Council of the Presbyterian Alliance which met in Philadelphia in September, 1880. He published in 1861 a Grammar of the Hebrew Language; in 1863, a Hebrew Chrestomathy; in 1866, an Elementary Hebrew Grammar; in 1863, "The Pentateuch Vindicated from the Aspersions of Bishop Colenso," and in 1870 he translated Zockler's "Commentary on the Song of Solomon," for the American edition of Lange's Commentary. He has also been a frequent contributor to the *Princeton Review* and to its successor, the *Presbyterian and Reformed Review.*

But probably he has in nothing rendered more efficient service for the Church and for the truth of God than in his opposition to the efforts to destroy confidence in the infallibility and absolute truthfulness of the Bible, made by that school of critics of which Dr. Briggs is the best-known leader in this country. His scholarship met and defeated them at every turn, and also strengthened the confidence of the people in the Word of God. To him evangelical Christians of all denominations owe a lasting debt of gratitude. In addition to a number of able review articles in defence of the Bible as it is and has been held by the Presbyterian and all other orthodox denominations, he has written several volumes distinguished for vast learning and great ability. Among these are "The Higher Criticism of the Pentateuch" and "The Unity of the Book of Genesis."

Christian Work of April 23, 1896.

Among the various semi-centennials that come trooping along, none, perhaps, will be celebrated with heartier enthusiasm than the fifty-year anniversary of the appointment of Professor William Henry Green to be Instructor in Princeton Theological Seminary. Fifty years is a long period to look back upon; for Professor Green it is a most memorable and inspiring period, for it speaks of noble work grandly performed. It was in 1846 that Professor Green first began to instruct the young theologues of Princeton, many of them now gray-headed men in the ministry of the Presbyterian Church. And though his teaching was interrupted by a pastorate in Philadelphia, it was only for two years. Since 1851 Professor Green has held the chair of Biblical and Oriental Literature in Princeton Theological Seminary; and how admirably his work has been done the world of church scholarship knows, for Professor Green's reputation is not confined to this country. Although in his scholarship Dr. Green is a pronounced conservative, he has always had the hearty respect and goodwill of the more radical element; for Dr. Green has always held his mind open to truth from any and every source; and if he has differed with many Biblical scholars, such as Dr. Harper and Professor Francis Brown and others, as to the origin and date of the Biblical books, he has arrived at his conclusions by a utilizing of the higher critical methods—the very methods adopted by his opponents. Indeed, not the least valuable service which Professor Green has rendered the Presbyterian Church—however slow some Presbyterian ministers are to perceive it—is his demonstration that not only is the higher criticism not the bugbear that some regard it as being, but rightly used it can be made a powerful method for defending the more conservative position. And it is safe to say that had Dr. Green not used this method, he would not stand as high in the estimation of Biblical scholars as he does to-day. We rejoice that the coming semi-centennial of Dr. Green's professional service is to be so worthily commemorated, in doing which the Presbyterian Church honors itself quite as much as it does the distinguished recipient of its regard.

The Presbyterian of April 29, 1896.

PRINCETON AND DR. GREEN.

Nearly a quarter of a century ago there was a " high day " in Princeton, N. J. It was the day when the fiftieth anniversary of the election of Dr. Charles Hodge to a professorship in the Theological Seminary of that place was celebrated by an assemblage such as had never gathered there before, and by services of a character which a few still living delight to recall. What was said in public is on record, and the generations to come may read therein what was thought of that good man and that great divine by the men who lived with him and saw the order and beauty of his daily life. What was said in private was said even more generously, but not less sincerely, and was the free expression of special esteem and love for the one whom all were striving to honor.

The writer of this article often recalls one of the private loving testimonies to Dr. Hodge which was uttered that day, and in a way which was to him very impressive. He was walking for a time, under the shade of the old trees in the front of North College, with the late Dr. Shedd, of Union Seminary, in New York City. We talked of other things for a few minutes, but our talk turned very soon to the day and to the occasion which had brought us there. Dr. Shedd paused at length in the conversation and his thoughts seemed to drift away into the past. Then, turning his fine, serious face around and looking upon the buildings and over the greensward before him, he said: "Yes, colleges like this *cost*. They take time; they call for self-denial; they demand lives consecrated to their service. But they pay—sometimes pay largely, and pay all at once. Princeton College gave back to the Church and the State a fine interest on all that is invested here when it produced such a man as *Charles Hodge.*" Dr. Shedd did not speak in public on that day, as Union Seminary was represented by his noble colleague, Dr. Henry B. Smith. We are very glad to make this late record of what he said so emphatically in private.

The biographer of Dr. Hodge has informed us that the suggestion of that celebration "originated with and its execution for the most part devolved upon his loving and filial pupil and colleague, Professor William H. Green." Now Princeton Seminary, with her roll of students, lengthened by the lapse of almost a quarter of a century, is about to do honor to one who has added lustre to the name of Princeton by giving his life to the training of young men for the high office of the ministry and to learned defences of the faith inherited from those fathers who laid deep the foundations of this institution. It is meet that such honor should be done to a man who has sought nothing for himself, but has given freely all his wealth of learning, his fine critical powers, and his wisdom in counsel to the service of the Church. In view of the celebration now close at hand, we may be permitted to give a brief sketch of the life and work of this most worthy man. . . .

In the "still air of delightful studies," and surrounded by the quiet beauty of his home in Princeton, Dr. Green has passed a long, laborious, and most useful life. Those who have been near him know how full this life has been of all that becomes a teacher, a student, a guide in the preparation for the highest of all offices, a citizen of the State, and a minister of the Gospel of Christ to his fellow-man. But those who know him best will be most ready to say that we will miss a most shining quality in the man if we did not say that he adds to great learning and abiding fidelity to truth the rarest and truest modesty. This is the crowning grace in a character which has won for Dr. Green the confidence and admiration of troops of friends, many of whom will gather next week in Princeton to give utterance to their loving appreciation of their old companion and teacher.

The New York Observer of April 30, 1896.

PROFESSOR WILLIAM HENRY GREEN.

The Theological Seminary of the Presbyterian Church, located at Princeton, N. J., has been fortunate in enjoying the services of several of its eminent professors during unusually long periods. Dr. Archibald Alexander and Dr. Samuel Miller constituted its first Faculty of instruction, and each of them was a professor for nearly forty years. Dr. Charles Hodge was the next addition to the teaching staff. He began to teach in 1820, and fifty-eight years later died as Professor of Exegetical, Didactic. and Polemic Theology. No later instructor has had a career as long as that, during which Dr. Hodge did so much to advance theological science and to promote the interests of Christian union and evangelical belief. But the brilliant Joseph Addison Alexander taught in its lecture-rooms for twenty-seven years (1833–60); Dr. A. T. McGill, the eminent father of the present Chancellor of New Jersey, was a member of the Faculty for thirty-five years (1854–89); Dr. Caspar Wistar Hodge, one of the best furnished and most inspiring teachers in New Testament history and exposition the country has produced, lectured on these subjects for thirty-one years (1860–91); and Dr. James Clement Moffatt, after a brilliant career as professor at Lafayette College, Miami University, and Princeton College, was Professor of Church History for twenty-nine years (1861–90).

The authorities of the Seminary are preparing to celebrate at the next commencement, on the 5th of the coming May, the accession to its teaching staff of the Rev. Dr. William Henry Green, now Professor of Oriental and Old Testament Literature. Dr. Green was appointed Instructor of Hebrew at Princeton a half century ago. How well he deserves this special recognition of his distinguished career is evident from the following sketch:

William Henry Green was born at Groveville, N. J., January 27, 1825. He belongs to a family that has occupied a conspicuous place in that State. His father was an eminent merchant. One of his uncles was Chancellor of New Jersey and another was Judge of the Court of Errors and Appeals. The eldest of his father's brothers was the late John C. Green, of New York, to whom Princeton College is indebted for its library and its school of science, Lawrenceville for its revived and enlarged preparatory school, and the College and Theological Seminary at Princeton for large endowments. Dr. Green is a descendant of Jonathan Dickinson, the first President of the College, and almost the first large gift of his uncle to the College was the building for lectures known as Dickinson Hall.

Though thus closely associated with New Jersey, he received his collegiate education in Pennsylvania. He was graduated with honors at Lafayette College, in 1840, before he was sixteen years old. He was made a tutor in his *alma mater* immediately upon his graduation, and held that position for two years, at an age when most boys are in preparatory schools. He resigned his tutorship in 1842, being only seventeen and a half years old, and matriculated as a student of theology at Princeton. Here he remained a year only; for Lafayette College needed his services again as teacher of mathematics, and he returned to Easton in that capacity. After a year's labors he came back to the Theological Seminary and completed the course, being graduated in 1846. By this time his theological *alma mater* felt that his services belonged to her. Dr. J. Addison Alexander was engaged in literary work, which all were convinced he should have the time to carry forward. Mr. Green's high character, scholarly habits, and remarkable powers of acquisition, especially in the sphere of languages, had attracted the attention of the Faculty, and he had shown, even as a boy of between fifteen and sixteen, that he could teach successfully minds as mature as those of college students. He was appointed Instructor of Hebrew, and continued in this position for three years. Meanwhile the Second Presbyterian Church of Princeton had been organized, and he added to the duties of Instructor in the Seminary those of the Church's stated supply.

He had been engaged in this work only a short time when his ability and fervor as a preacher attracted the attention of several Presbyterian churches. It became a serious question, whether one with his preaching gifts ought to remain in a small village, even though engaged in work as useful as that of an Instructor in Hebrew. This question seemed to him and to the Church to have been answered permanently, when in 1849, at twenty-four years of age, after having taught higher branches of learning six years, he accepted a call to one of the most influential Presbyterian churches of Philadelphia, the Central Church. There are some still living on whose minds and hearts his preaching made a profound impression. He was recognized as one of the ablest and most acceptable preachers in Philadelphia at a time when Albert Barnes and Henry A. Boardman and Charles Wadsworth and Charles W. Shields were among its Presbyterian pastors; and though he was above all a student, and had the diffidence in society of a man of books, his congregation found him a laborious, faithful, and sympathetic pastor. About thirty years ago one of his students, meeting him at an evening reception and impressed with the difference between the immediate circumstances of their association and those of their daily encounters in the "Miller Lecture-Room," greeted him with the remark: "Dr. Green, I am delighted to meet you. so to say, on English ground." All the accounts of his brief pastorate justify the conclusion that to meet him on "English ground" and as a pastor was a most pleasant experience. There was no department of the pastor's work in which he was not successful. Ten years after its close one of the students of the Seminary, who was in a position to know, said to the writer of this sketch: "I do not believe that there is in New Jersey a more acceptable speaker to children than Rabbi Green."

From this pastorate, two years after its commencement, the General Assembly of the Presbyterian Church called him to the chair of Biblical and Oriental Literature in Princeton Seminary. The same Assembly transferred Dr. Addison Alexander to the chair of Biblical and Ecclesiastical History. The Seminary was entering upon the second stage in its history. Dr. Miller died in 1850 and Dr. Archibald Alexander in 1851, the year of Professor Green's election. During the same year the Seminary lost Dr. James W. Alexander, who became the pastor of what is now known as the Fifth Avenue Presbyterian Church of New York City. Between 1851 and 1854, when Dr. McGill was elected, Dr. Hodge, Dr. Addison Alexander, and Professor Green were the Faculty.

Professor Green, notwithstanding the administrative work that was necessarily added to his new duties, not only gave elementary and advanced instruction in Hebrew, and prepared his courses in general and special Introduction, but became a frequent contributor to the *Biblical Repertory* and other journals, writing for the most part on Old Testament and philological subjects.

. . . .

Soon after he became Professor in the Seminary he felt the need of a new Hebrew grammar, and set himself to the task of its preparation. The first edition appeared in 1861, and the fourth edition in 1885, to which he subsequently added a complete syntax. A Hebrew Chrestomathy was published in 1863, and an Elementary Grammar in 1866, a new edition appearing in 1871. A large proportion of the articles whose titles have been given were written in defence of the Scriptures and against special attacks. Soon after the publication of the grammar the excitement caused by Bishop Colenso's attack upon the trustworthiness of the Mosaic history led Dr. Green to defend it in a small, but spirited, volume, entitled "The Pentateuch Vindicated from the Aspersions of Bishop Colenso." He took part in the preparation of the American edition of Lange's Commentary, being the translator and editor of Zöckler's " Commentary on the Song of Solomon."

When the American Company for the Anglo-American Bible Revision Committee was organized some time in the seventies, Dr. Green's high position among American scholars was so generally recognized that he was elected Chairman of the Old Testament Section. It is understood that the traits of this revision, which have pleased the conservative and called out the criticism of the more nearly "radical" Hebraists, from the beginning received his cordial approval. At all events, Dr. Green, when the critics had delivered themselves, came to the defence of the Old Testament revision, and made a positive attack on the critics in an article as "vivacious" (as Matthew Arnold would have said) as anything he had written since his volume on Bishop Colenso. While engaged with his colleagues in the work of revising the English version of the Old Testament, he published a volume of expository lectures, with the title, "The Argument of the Book of Job Unfolded."

Meanwhile events occurred within a sister Presbyterian Church and in his own Church which led to new literary activity. The scholars of the Congregational and Presbyterian Churches in America, until lately, have been slow to make concessions in controversies which involve the authenticity of the Scriptures or the trustworthiness of their historical sections. Perhaps the general attitude of American scholars is nowhere better exemplified than in the writings of one of the largest-minded, most catholic, and most generously cultivated theological scholars America has produced, the late Dr. Henry B. Smith, of Union Theological Seminary. Let any one take up his volume of essays, called "Faith and Philosophy," and his "Apologetics," and he will see what we mean by his attitude. Strauss, Renan, the essays and reviews, agnosticism, relativity of knowledge, are attacked with vigor, and always from the point of view of profound faith in the historical trustworthiness of the Bible and the reality of a supernatural revelation authenticated by miracles. But there has lately been manifested in Presbyterian Scotland and in American Presbyterianism a strong disposition not only to concede in apologetics, but to treat concessiveness as a note of scholarship. This disposition has shown itself notably in Biblical discussions, and most notably in discussions concerning the Old Testament. Along with this has appeared what is scarcely exaggeration to describe as a tendency to solve critical questions by counting scholarly noses; and the rule has appeared to prevail that, if the nose has a German owner, even if the owner should be only a *privat docent*, it ought rightfully to be counted as at least two.

Dr. Green's attitude in this controversy has been precisely like the attitude of Dr. Henry B. Smith in the controversies in which he appeared as a Christian apologist. Christian scholarship loses none of its scholarly quality by being joined to profound Christian conviction. Indeed, in these Old Testament discussions Dr. Green's scholarship has been strikingly exhibited. For he has not been exposed, as those on the other side have been, to the temptation to which some of them have yielded; the temptation, namely, to substitute easier reportorial work for serious and original investigation. Whatever may be said of the present state or of the probable outcome of the discussion, the contributions made to it by Dr. Green are strongly marked by the qualities derived from earnest and thorough and independent study of the questions in debate. He was one of the first to appear in defence of the truthfulness of the Old Testament history after the publication of Professor W. Robertson Smith's lectures. Besides his contributions to the periodical press, he has published four volumes on the Old Testament controversy, "Moses and the Prophets," "The Hebrew Feasts," "The Higher Criticism of the Pentateuch," and "The Unity of the Book of Genesis." It does not fall within the scope of this paper to review or even to characterize these volumes. That may well be left to the experts. But we cannot leave them without two remarks. The first is that in these volumes the American Church has met the attacks lately made on the trustworthiness of the Bible with as much vigor and ability as she has ever displayed in resisting attacks upon her faith. The other is that, if at the close of the present controversy the American Churches shall retain their faith in the Old Testament history, they will be likely to regard Dr. Green more than any other scholar as their foremost representative in the conflict.

We have little space left in which to speak of Dr. Green as a teacher. His pupils will all remember him as always thoroughly in earnest, always clear, always strong, always under the sway of a sense of duty, always ready to work to the point of exhaustion, and always demanding sincere and sufficient work from his class. Partly because of the seriousness of his manner, and partly because of the strained attention which the subject and the teacher united in exacting, the most of his pupils have at first regarded him with a feeling of awe akin to fear. Many a student, during Dr. Green's earlier and middle career, has felt that in his class-room, certainly, the students were not " under grace," but " under law." It appeared to many of them that the elder dispensation had indeed been revived. Not a few of his pupils, in moments of confidential intercourse, have whispered to their fellows that this was their feeling. But no teacher has enjoyed more unanimously or more profoundly the respect of all he has taught. No theological teacher has held steadily before his pupils by word and life a higher ideal of the student's and the minister's calling, or impressed it upon them more strongly and abidingly. And in all he has taught he has been as clear and strong and scholarly as any teacher Princeton has ever had. No one of all the succession from Archibald Alexander onward has enjoyed a larger measure of respect.

And whenever any student for any worthy reason has been brought into personal contact with Dr. Green, especially if he has happened to be in perplexity or sorrow of any kind, there has been added to this high respect an affection for whose expression the student has always wished only the opportunity. We venture to say that pride in Dr. Green's ability and attainments and respect for his lofty, sincere, and simple character are not more profound or general among his students than affection for a personality as modest, as gentle, as sympathetic, and every way as engaging as that of any theological teacher in the country.

We congratulate the large body of his indebted students on the opportunity afforded them by the coming celebration to give expression to their pride, their respect, and their love. We congratulate the Christian Church and the American State on his long and eminent career. We congratulate the Presbyterian Church for this new opportunity to honor a clergyman on whom it has already conferred its highest official dignity. We congratulate Princeton University that it is permitted to send its greetings to the eminent scholar whom it once called to its Presidency. We congratulate Dr. Green on the distinguished services he has been able to render to learning and to truth ; and on the love, and the honor, and the troops of friends that are his to-day. *Serus in cælum redeat!*

The Evangelist of April 30, 1896.
PROFESSOR WILLIAM HENRY GREEN'S JUBILEE.

Fifty years of active scholarly life are not given to many men, though we believe that the continuous employment of the mind and heart on the greatest subjects is conducive to longevity. One who has given the subject special attention tells us that the necrological list published annually in the minutes of the General Assembly testifies every year to the long life in the land of those who, in the Presbyterian Church, as pastors, missionaries, and professors are, at least by the character of their work, removed measurably from the feverish strife after material things, and compelled to think of the things that are unseen and eternal. Only a week or two ago we extended our congratulations to our beloved brother and contributor, Theodore Ledyard Cuyler, on the completion of his half century of clerical and literary labors, and we have now great pleasure in offering congratulations of a like character to one whose work, though somewhat different, has had in view the advancement of the same high interests, and has been performed with a like sincerity and a like loyalty to the vision of the truth vouchsafed him. We are led thus to unite the names of Dr. Theodore L. Cuyler and Dr. William Henry Green, not only because their labors have covered the same period, and because they are both men of high character, but also because they were fellow-students at Princeton Theological Seminary.

The great divines of the earlier periods of the Congregational and Presbyterian Churches in this country were above all systematic theologians. The discussions which agitated these communions during the last century and the earlier half of the present century, were within the limits of dogmatics. With what earnestness of purpose the great New England ministers of that whole period gave themselves to the study of the *loci communes* of the reformed theology, and with what ability and spirit they either expounded and defended their "improvements of Calvinism," or resisted them and vindicated the elder views ! The day will never come when the names of these men will not be mentioned with profound respect. They are venerable and renowned—John Norton, of Ipswich, Mass. ; Willard, President of Harvard ; the two Presidents Edwards, father and son ; Bellamy, Smalley, Samuel Hopkins, Nathaniel Emmons, Timothy Dwight, and, though the first President of Princeton College, a New England man by birth and education (an ancestor, too, of the subject of this editorial), Jonathan Dickinson, of Elizabethtown, N. J. It was on theological grounds that the Congregational Churches were divided into two communions, that the Plan of Union between Congregationalism and Presbyterianism was formed and afterward abrogated, and that the Presbyterian Church in 1837 became two bodies.

But early in the present century there were indications that there would be a change in the central subject of theological study and debate; that Biblical questions would become the burning questions among our scholars. As the century passed beyond its first third, these indications became more marked. By that time Biblical scholars like Moses Stuart, of Andover; Andrews Norton, of Cambridge Divinity School, and Addison Alexander, of Princeton, were attracting increased attention from the ministers of the country. Edward Robinson was making plans for his Palestinian researches, and George Bush and Albert Barnes were preparing their popular commentaries. As we can now see, a movement was taking place which, before the close of the century, would distribute parties in the Churches upon entirely new lines, would give a new character to the preaching of the ministers, and create a new literature for the shelves of pastors' libraries. It is difficult for one under fifty years of age to appreciate the change in sermon, library, debate, and ecclesiastical parties, which has resulted from the revival of Biblical study, to which we have briefly referred. The importance of the celebration of Dr. Green's fifty years of active labor as a Biblical scholar, writer, and teacher is due, in part at least, to the fact that he is one of the oldest scholars, and one of the most eminent as well, who have promoted this revival. . . .

Dr. Green's charming simplicity and sincerity of character have won for him the love of many generations of students, counting a class as a generation. All of them speak of him with enthusiasm as a teacher, all venerate him as a great and good man, and all love him as their friend. Fortunate is the teacher who, as he approaches the close of a long and great career, can gather about him so many hundreds whom he has inspired and instructed as Dr. Green will have around him on May 5th. There is no higher kind of joy than his will be, when, on that day, pastors and missionaries and teachers, from all over the world, will give expression to their gratitude for his high teaching and high example. Besides these will come his co-laborers in other institutions, representatives from the College at which he was graduated, and from the College in Princeton of which he has so long been a Trustee. *The Evangelist* gladly anticipates them in their congratulations, their eulogies, and their best wishes, and cordially offers its tribute to the great Biblical scholar, the eminent divine, the able apologist, the honored theological teacher, but, above all, to the noble, simple, sincere, and modest Christian man.

The Presbyterian Journal of April 30, 1896.

THE CELEBRATION AT PRINCETON SEMINARY.

We take great pleasure in calling attention to the great teacher and divine, the fiftieth anniversary of whose connection as a theological Instructor with Princeton Seminary is so soon to be celebrated.

Dr. William Henry Green has had an exceptional career. He was only fifteen when he was graduated at Lafayette College. He had achieved high honors as a student, and the College at once employed him as a tutor. Two years later he began to study for the ministry, but a year only had been passed in the Seminary when he was called again to Easton to teach mathematics. At the close of another year he was back at Princeton, where he completed his theological course without further interruption. The Seminary now made him Instructor in Hebrew. This was fifty years ago, and he was not yet twenty-two years old. The Second Church, in Princeton, had just been organized, and he preached statedly in its pulpit while performing the duties of his chair. His earnest and able preaching led to calls from several prominent churches, and when he was twenty-four he accepted the invitation to the pulpit of the Central Church, Philadelphia. Two years later the General Assembly sent him back to Princeton to fill the chair of Old Testament and Oriental Literature. From that time on he has lived in Princeton and filled this professorship, with what ability and fidelity and signal success both the Church and the world of Old Testament scholars know.

The rapid development of his powers as a teacher, preacher, and student was, of course, exceptional, but so healthy was it that, so far as we are aware, it never excited the fear of those who knew him that it would be followed by a brief and unfruitful period of activity. The old *Biblical Repertory* opened its pages to him, and his studies furnished him subjects. Between 1851 and 1867 he wrote for it forty-one articles on a variety of themes, which no one could have embraced who was not endowed with remarkable gifts, and who had not made great attainments in his department. Besides these he wrote during the same period a number of papers for philological journals. These were the fruit of constant thought and study in the sphere of language. Meanwhile he was active as preacher and professor and in the administration of the Seminary. All who were brought into contact with him, whether as students, or colleagues, or hearers, respected his high and sincere character, his gifts, and learning. He made his students work hard, for he worked hard himself; and he impressed upon them a faith in the elder revelation like that which he himself enjoyed. . . .

His life has been a full one. It would be hard to exaggerate the importance of the work he has done. He has the highest respect of the entire Church, and his students will gather in great numbers to testify not only their respect, but their deep and warm affection on May 5th next. Such a celebration has special significance. We are often told that ours is a material age and that we are a materialized people, but the wide interest which the proposal thus to honor this modest scholar and divine has awakened shows that there is a large proportion of the people of the United States not wholly given to the seen and the temporal.

The Presbyterian Messenger of April 30, 1896.

DR. GREEN'S JUBILEE.

As already announced in these columns, it is the intention of the Directors of Princeton Seminary to celebrate on May 5th the fiftieth anniversary of the appointment of Professor William Henry Green as an Instructor in that institution, and the approach of the day makes it appropriate for his many admirers, even outside of the ranks of the Princeton Alumni, to give expression to their sense of the high degree in which Dr. Green has merited such a celebration.

The Alumni of Princeton Seminary, scattered throughout the world, will turn their thoughts with especial affection on next Tuesday to their *alma mater*, and will do honor, with one consent, to their beloved and famous teacher. They may well do so. Few of them now remain who have not sat at his feet. They know that his great learning has been devoted to their interests and to the increase of their usefulness in the kingdom of God. We doubt not that they are ready to thank him even for the hard lessons he imposed on minds not accustomed to oriental tongues; but certainly they are ready to thank God for the work which he has done in defence of the Scriptures and for the influence which his name has given to their Seminary. We do not grudge them the natural pride in the possession of one whose long career as a teacher has been distinguished by scholarship of the first rank, and withal by a simple-hearted love of truth and a genial disposition, which has made him loved as well as honored by the many pupils who have come under his care.

Dr. Green, however, belongs to the whole Church as well as to Princeton Seminary. As Moderator of the General Assembly in 1891 he received the highest honor in the gift of his denomination. As a leading member of the American Revision Committee he did valuable service for all readers and students of the English Bible. His contributions to the critical study of the Old Testament have given him still greater prominence, especially since criticism has busied itself with that portion of the Bible. Whatever critical opinions men may have—whether they adopt the new views or, with Dr. Green, defend the old—they must acknowledge at once his scholarship and his candor. His books are models of critical argument. They evince entire familiarity with opposing views and perfect fairness in representing them. Dr. Green never rests his case on rhetoric nor supports it by trivial reason. He is solid, thorough, learned, and honest. He is to-day the leading champion in the world of the traditional view of the Old Testament. Hence we take pleasure in uniting with Princeton Alumni in tendering him our cordial congratulations and in the prayer that he may yet be spared many years to the Seminary and the Church.

The Christian Intelligencer of May 6, 1896.

Professor Green, of Princeton, whose Jubilee as a teacher in Biblical literature is celebrated this week, has been a tower of strength to the thousands in evangelical churches who know from experience the value of the Bible and have been somewhat alarmed by the persistent assaults of the higher critics. Their faith has been supported by the knowledge that Dr. Green believed that Moses wrote the Pentateuch, David the Psalms ascribed to him, and other authors the books which bear their names. They knew that Dr. Green was as good a scholar as the higher critics, and a great deal more sober, judicious, and trustworthy than many of those whose speculations he rejected, and it was enough for them that he found no reason for accepting the destructive higher criticism. There are thousands of Christians throughout the country who thank God to-day for Dr. Green.

The Watchman (Boston) of May 7, 1896.

The fiftieth anniversary of the connection of Professor William H. Green with the Hebrew department of Princeton Theological Seminary is to be appropriately celebrated this week. In another column we review his last theological work. Professor Green stands at the very head of Hebrew scholars in this country, and he has a very high reputation in Europe. Like our own Professor Osgood, he has never been carried away by the theories of the "Higher Criticism," and has brought to the defence of conservative views of the Scriptures enormous learning and singular argumentative power. A few years ago Professor Green, at our request, contributed to these columns a series of articles on the new critical theories, which were at once recognized as masterly and convincing. This is the kind of work, in addition to the duties of his chair, that he has been doing through all the years. The Presbyterian Church does well to honor a scholar who has stood like a breakwater against the advancing tide of critical novelties. In his defence of conservative views of the Scriptures Professor Green has often been charged with a controlling prejudice in favor of the received opinions. His opponents, however, assume that they discuss these great questions with perfectly candid and open minds. There could not be a greater mistake. Nothing can be plainer than that, to quote the language of Professor George P. Fisher, who certainly is not a purblind traditionalist, "a great deal of the current criticism of the historical writings of the Bible is affected by a pre-existing bias against the supernatural element in these narratives. There is at the start a prejudice which warps the judgment respecting their date and authorship and general credibility."

The Presbyterian of May 13, 1896.

PRINCETON DOING HONOR TO DR. GREEN.

[EDITORIAL CORRESPONDENCE.]

The close of the term at the Theological Seminary in Princeton had this year an additional interest because of its association with the fiftieth anniversary of the election of the Rev. William Henry Green to a professorship in the institution. When we reached the chapel that morning the services connected with the graduation of more than seventy young men were well over, and large groups of black-coated men were scattered round, awaiting the signal to fall into line and march to Alexander Hall, on the College grounds, where the Jubilee services were appointed to be held. Within the chapel, we were told, the simple services accompanying the dismissal of the senior class to the great field for which they had been preparing, had been held. The last hymn had been sung by the members of the class, and words of wise and cheerful counsel had been spoken to them by Dr. George D. Baker, of Philadelphia, as the representative of the Board of Directors. These exercises were begun early, and were made somewhat briefer than usual that the day might be given to a service such as Princeton has not seen since that April day in the year 1872, when good men and men of renown in theological circles gathered together there to do honor to the long and faithful work wrought in the same institution and for the same space of time by Dr. Charles Hodge.

To one who was a spectator on both these remarkable occasions it seemed that the only change visible was that Princeton has grown seemingly more academic in her ways than she was in the former days. The black gowns and the mortar-board caps were very abundant in the company this year, and here and there a doctor's hood of buff or scarlet, intermingled with ribbons of blue, gave variety to the scene. The procession took its way, in quiet and sedate fashion, to the College grounds ʻ d filed into the new and spacious Commencement Hall, which b..rs the name of Alexander. The wide galleries were filled by ladies, who had been there awaiting our coming. The audience soon settled down in their places in the great, beautiful, roomy hall, and Rev. Dr. Gosman sat in the marble chair, over which is thrown a canopy, as the presiding officer of the occasion. Very soon the venerable form of Dr. William Henry Green was seen slowly making his way to his chair in the front. As he came near, the whole assembly rose, and a great cheer went up, or went round. The guest of the day was in the midst of the company of his pupils and friends. There was something of weakness in his step, and there was more than usual pallor on the cheek, but the face and the form were those well known to the successive generations of students before whom he had walked and unto whom he had "opened the Scriptures." The hymn, "I love Thy Kingdom, Lord," was sung, a very suitable prayer offered by Dr. Lansing, of the New Brunswick Seminary, and Dr. Gosman then very fitly introduced, in a brief address, the services of the day, and gave utterance to the strong confidence and abiding love felt for Dr. Green in the various Boards which control the Seminary.

We cannot follow the various speakers of the morning in the addresses in which they rehearsed the work of Dr. Green's life and gathered up the results of his long career of study and instruction. Dr. Mead, of Hartford Theological Seminary, gave us a very careful estimate of the value of Dr. Green's critical labors, especially in his masterly dealing with the various phases of the divisive and conjectural criticism of the Old Testament, which furnishes so many of the burning questions of the times. Here Dr. Green's unquestioned scholarship in all that pertains to Biblical criticism gave him the place of one who spoke by authority. His position was always up among the first; and Dr. Mead closed his fine and most discriminating tribute to the Professor with the measured words: "It cannot be doubted that among the higher critics who, with patient toil and profound scholarship, lead in the maintenance of sound views of the Bible and aim to strengthen the foundations of a reasonable faith, will always stand the name of William Henry Green."

Dr. Mead was followed by Dr. McCurdy, of Montreal, who is a son of Princeton, and a pupil, in former days, of Dr. Green. His task was to assign Dr. Green's place in "Semitic Scholarship," and to describe the methods by which Hebrew was taught in the Seminary in past years. His opening sentence is worthy of quotation: "It is a great thing to have been a teacher fifty years; it is greater to have been a teacher in Princeton Seminary for so long a time, and it is greater still to have been a teacher of Hebrew. For Hebrew lies at the bottom of things—at least, of the things which are worth most at Princeton."

President Patton, of Princeton College, came forward when Dr. McCurdy had closed, and the applause which greeted him was hearty and long continued. The high-water mark of sincere and affectionate eulogy was reached when Dr. Patton said, in one of the earliest of his sentences: " I am glad to stand here to do honor to a man whom I venerate *as I venerate no other living man.*" That sentence went to the heart of the great audience. It quickened, while it fittingly expressed the reverential feelings of hundreds of men sitting before him, many of them in the midst of life's toils or going down to old age, who had sat in their youth at the feet of this master in sacred learning. Dr. Patton's speech was very suggestive and incisive, as his manner of speech always is. When it closed the applause was loud and long.

Ere it was hushed Dr. Green was on his feet. We had hardly dared to hope that his voice would be heard, save in brief acknowledgment of the honors done to him. But his first words reassured us. We listened to the old and well-remembered tones. "Fellow-Alumni," said he, and we rose to our feet to greet him, and stood while his first sentences were spoken. Thankfulness for the tributes paid to him, and modest acceptance of the kindly words spoken of him and of his work, accompanied by a re-assertion of the old position of Princeton Seminary in regard to the Word of God, were the salient points of his speech, and he closed by expressing his firm faith in the future of the venerable Seminary, and then, looking round, said : " May the Word of God, my dear friends, abide in you, and crown you all with its richest blessings."

Following this most affecting scene were words of congratulation and of kindly interest from representatives of other institutions, colleges, universities, and theological schools. Dr. Booth, the Moderator of the General Assembly, as was fit, pronounced words of commendation upon the long work of this faithful servant of the whole Church. "The Church," said Dr. Booth, "which knows its own mind and clings to its Bible." The benediction of the Southern Presbyterian Church was not withheld from one who had assisted to train many of its ministers, and it was brought by Dr. McPheeters, of the Columbia Seminary. This was a most grateful feature of this happy occasion. Dr. Warfield, President of Lafayette College, spoke for the College and in recognition of the services of its distinguished graduate ; and the Trustees of Princeton University were represented by Henry M. Alexander, LL.D., of New York City, who claimed to be there from hereditary right. He said to Dr. Green that he was " instructed by the Trustees of the University to express their admiration of your character and achievements and the hope that you may continue to add glory to your own name and that of Princeton Seminary."

The final congratulatory address came from a representative of a committee which had done its work and ceased to be, but of which Dr. Green had been a conspicuous member. The Committee of American Scholars, who had in charge the revision of the Old Testament Scriptures, made Dr. Green their Chairman, and Dr. Howard Osgood, Professor in Rochester University and a member of that committee, told us of the ease and courtesy with which he presided over the long deliberation of the committee, and the respectful attention which was always given to his suggestions by its members.

A lunch was served at University Hotel, and the afternoon was spent in listening to reminiscences of Dr. Green in his youth and his maturer years. Dr. Cattell, ex-President of Lafayette College, opened the speaking in the afternoon, which was somewhat less formal than in the morning. Dr. Cattell described Dr. Green as the young collegian who read much, was not severely studious, and was ready generally for a game of chess, but who was found always at the head of the class. Dr. Cuyler, of Brooklyn, followed with reminiscences of " Dr. Green as a Classmate," recalling him as a tall, modest, manly youth, twenty years of age, who "took to Greek as if he had been born in Athens, and to Hebrew as if he had been the son of a rabbi in Jerusalem." The reminiscences of Dr. A. A. E. Taylor, of Columbus, O., were given in connection with the theme, "The Young Professor." In his first years the youthful teacher had to face such men as were afterward known as Dr. Robert Watts, of Belfast; Dr. James P. Boyce, of South Carolina; Caspar Wistar Hodge, afterward Professor in the Seminary, and Isadore Loewenthal, the learned Jewish convert, who died in India. He proved equal to the task which he had accepted. Dr. Griffin, of Johns Hopkins University, in Baltimore, came next, speaking of "The Established Teacher," and Rev. Dr. John Fox, of Brooklyn, of "The Learned Doctor." The whole service was brought back into the closeness and intimacy of a family circle, when Dr. William M. Paxton concluded all the words of reverence and loyalty which have been laid at Dr. Green's feet by an affectionate description of the man and the scholar as the President of the Faculty of the Seminary. Then, rising, the great assembly received the benediction from the lips of Canon Mason, Professor of Divinity in the University of Cambridge, England.

We left Princeton as the shadows of the evening were falling, thankful for the day of enjoyment, thankful for the institution which has grown into such strength and usefulness, and thankful that we had been permitted to witness the close of a half century of devout and conscientious service rendered to the beloved Seminary by such men as Charles Hodge and William Henry Green.

The New York Observer of May 14, 1896.

PRINCETON HONORS DR. GREEN.

Tuesday, May 5th, was a high day at Princeton, and a memorable one for the whole Presbyterian Church. The occasion was the eighty-fourth commencement of the Theological Seminary, and the fiftieth anniversary of the appointment of William Henry Green, D.D., LL.D., as Instructor. To Princeton the tribes of attached Alumni and visiting friends went up in full force. Quantity and quality were there. All day Monday multitudes of visitors kept coming in, and on Tuesday itself special trains ran to accommodate the throng. Though the numerous black coats of the visiting clergy tended to give a sombre aspect to affairs, the occasion was not at all a gloomy one. It was a festival, not a funeral.

At 9 A.M. the closing exercises of the Theological Seminary were held in the Miller Chapel. The Rev. Dr. George D. Baker, of Philadelphia, in very manly and earnest fashion, made a brief address to the graduates. Diplomas were then distributed, and while seventy-eight members of the graduating class remained standing in front of the platform, the Rev. Dr. William M. Paxton addressed them on behalf of the Faculty, pointing out that the life of the minister was largely his sermon, and reminiscently quoting the counsel which he had received from the godly Samuel Miller. When a student about to take leave of the Seminary, Dr. Miller urged the young minister to do two things, at least—to keep near the throne of grace and to care for the children of his charge. The class hymn was then sung, a brief meeting of the Alumni held, and the procession formed preparatory to the exercises in Alexander Hall. Led by Rev. Dr. William M. Paxton, of the Seminary, and Rev. Dr. Robert Russell Booth, Moderator of the Presbyterian General Assembly, a long array of gowned notables, representatives of other institutions, alumni, trustees, professors, and students, to the number of about two thousand, proceeded in double column to Alexander Hall, moving at a slow and dignified pace, as though mindful of the Princeton principle to make speed slowly.

The scene in the beautiful and spacious Alexander Hall was most striking and memorable. On the platform were many men distinguished in ecclesiastical and educational spheres, among them the man whom all delighted to honor, and who received a perfect ovation as he took his seat at the right of the chairman. The galleries were brilliant with the bright costumes of the ladies, while the body of the house was monotonously black with the clerical costumes of the great mass of clergymen. When the vast audience joined in singing the grand old hymn, "I love Thy Kingdom, Lord," hearts as well as lips moved with unfeigned praise and worship. After prayer by the Rev. Dr. Lansing, of New Brunswick, the opening address was delivered by the venerable chairman, Dr. Abraham Gosman, President of the Board of Directors, dealing with Dr. Green's services to the Seminary. This was most appreciative in tone, concluding with the affectionate words: "Thanks, beloved teacher and friend!" The second address, by the Rev. Dr. Charles M. Mead, of the Hartford Theological Seminary, illustrated in clear and cogent style, by many examples, Dr. Green's contributions to Biblical criticism. Dr. Mead began by quoting the German adage, "Jubilations are tribulations," and added, with reference to the recipient of the congratulations of the day: "If he deprecates the praise, we will praise him all the more for his modesty." And surely, if Dr. Green were not a modest as well as a famous man, he would now be puffed up beyond measure, after all the commendations of his Jubilee day. Dr. Green, said the speaker, has an absolute confidence that out of the present indecisive condition of things would issue a final triumph for truth, and could afford to laugh at the pert critics who can find no "honest" criticism except in the case of the most radical investigators—critics who take the Pentateuch to pieces, and when the partition is completed, find that it corresponds to the hypotheses simply because it was made by the hypotheses. Dr. Green has made it certain, said Dr. Mead, that no one can be certain as to the authorship of an ancient writing when the sole means of judging lies in the writing itself, adding that the days of excessive radicalism are passing away, and that men now are less afraid than formerly of believing what their fathers believed.

The theme, "Dr. Green's Contribution to Semitic Scholarship," was treated of in an address, greatly enjoyed by the audience, delivered by the Rev. Dr. J. F. McCurdy, Professor in University College, Toronto, a former student of Princeton Seminary. Dr. McCurdy noted three eras in the history of Semitic instruction at Princeton—the first, that introduced by Dr. Charles Hodge himself; the second, the period connected with the name of Dr. J. Addison Alexander; and the third, the period of Dr. Green's thorough and brilliant labors. In his critical review of these eras the speaker was on delicate ground, but he handled the analysis well, as he made it leap up to a deserved tribute to Dr. Green, who had put the crown of a ripe and broadened scholarship on the necessarily incompleter labors of others in the particular field of Hebrew. Dr. Green, said Dr. McCurdy, was a scholar with whom philology was not a love of words, but of the Word.

To say that the address of President Patton, of Princeton University, was the address of the day would be an invidious reflection on many other fine speakers, but certainly no speaker moved the audience more than did he. Dr. Patton is always thoughtful, incisive, brilliant, but his address on this occasion seemed to awaken a feeling that does not always find expression in his apt, telling speech. The theme assigned the President of the University was that of Dr. Green's services to the Church at large. Dr. Patton, in his handling of it, very properly stretched it out beyond the bounds of Presbyterianism. He began by saying that he reverenced Dr. Green as he did no other living man. As for Princeton, when she ceases to be heard on burning questions that affect evangelical Christendom, her glory will pass away. Dr. Green was a thorough, painstaking scholar, who had narrowed his sphere of labor and thereby widened his influence —inasmuch as the best way for any man to serve the Church at large is to serve the Church to which he belongs. As a scholar Professor Green acted on the principle that the way to keep strong in the chair is to keep busy in the study; as a teacher he never read his Bible to his class with a shake of his head or a shrug of his shoulders. We have plenty of men, said Dr. Patton, who can handle ideas and manipulate notions, but what we need is men of minute and specialized learning. A reference was made, in passing, to the "complicated algebra" of Pentateuchal analysis.

And yet, said the speaker, Dr. Green has never taken the view that the defence against the higher criticism has no place in a theological seminary. He has not stopped to ask : " What would happen if the critics are right ? " but has addressed himself to the stupendous task of proving that the critics are wrong. There exists no necessity for a separated Pentateuch except that which seems to be created at the behest of a naturalistic philosophy. The concluding sentences of the address, to the effect that Dr. Green's book, "The Unity of Genesis," is his masterpiece in the forensic sphere, and puts its author in a foremost place among the few great apologists of the world, were greeted with most vigorous applause.

At this point the venerable subject of these eulogies came forward to acknowledge the compliments paid him, when immediately the great audience rose to its feet and remained standing as the learned professor expressed his gratitude in a few earnest sentences of grateful acknowledgment. Princeton, he said, does not shrink from the most rigorous tests of scholarship, but is confident that sound learning will ever go hand in hand with implicit faith in the sacred volume.

After Dr. Green had concluded his feeling remarks six congratulatory addresses were delivered by Rev. Robert Russell Booth, D.D., Moderator of the General Assembly, on behalf of the Presbyterian Church ; Dr. Wm. M. McPheeters, of Columbia Theological Seminary, on behalf of sister churches ; Dr. Willis J. Beecher, of Auburn Seminary, on behalf of sister seminaries ; President E. D. Warfield, of Lafayette College, who spoke for Dr. Green's *alma mater ;* Henry M. Alexander, LL.D., who represented the Trustees of Princeton College, and the Rev. Howard Osgood, of Rochester Theological Seminary, who had served with Dr. Green on the Old Testament Revision Committee. Dr. Booth declared that he offered heartfelt congratulations from the believing Presbyterian Church, which knows its own mind, and is aware of the difference between naturalism and supernaturalism, and that recognizes in Dr. Green in this emergency of scholarship a firm and successful defender of the truth. Dr. McPheeters thought that, if we were not opposed on principle to sacred places, Princeton might serve as a very fitting Mecca of Presbyterianism. The speaker alluded to Dr. Wm. Hayes Ward's estimate of Dr. Green as the most vigorous defender of the traditional views—a man who never mistook declamations for refutations, nor abuse for argument. Dr. Warfield spoke feelingly of Lafayette's continued love for her former pupil. Dr. Osgood said that out of thirteen years of discussion and conference relative to Old Testament questions no member of the Revision Committee, a committee composed of men of very positive and variant views, ever carried away the sting of a single discourteous remark or suggestion from Dr. Green, its chairman. At the conclusion of the congratulatory addresses reference was made to the pile, perhaps two feet high, of letters of reply received from institutions and individuals, both in Europe and America, expressing an interest in the occasion.

Adjournment was then had for dinner. At 3 P.M. was held a "reminiscence meeting." Dr. William C. Cattell, formerly President of Lafayette College, spoke of the "Father of the Man," and brought out the curious fact that the young William Henry Green when a student at Lafayette went to his instructor and desired to be excused from the study of languages, for which he said he had no aptitude! But no record exists of the fact that he ever sought to be excused from or ever missed college prayers, although these were then held at five o'clock in the morning. Dr. Theodore L. Cuyler then delivered a ringing speech on the theme, "Our Fellow Student," referring to Dr. Green as a man who took to Greek as though he had been born in Athens, and to Hebrew as though he were the son of a rabbi. Dr. A. A. E. Taylor, of Columbus, spoke of "The Young Professor," whose faculty of making a bee-line from his lecture-room to his study was prophetic of the direct methods of his dealing all through life—who had "no mania for hypotheses," and yet was actively constructive in his teachings. Dr. Edwin H. Griffin, Dean of Johns Hopkins University, eulogized "The Established Teacher," quoting, in connection with a reference to his spirit of conscientious scholarship, a remark of Dr. Hodge's, that "a knowledge of Greek grammar was the best preparation for heaven." Dr. John Fox, of Brooklyn, made some happy allusions to "The Learned Doctor," who had impressed the students who came in contact with him with a profounder sense of the real meaning of "sacred letters." Dr. William M. Paxton concluded the speeches with a very appreciative tribute to Dr. Green as "The Head of the Faculty," calling attention to the fact that the Princeton Seminary Faculty, all elect men in two senses—chosen both by Seminary and Assembly—were, with one exception, pupils of Dr. Green. The growth of Princeton Seminary was due largely to the fact that it had always stood for something definite in thought and doctrine, and had been greatly contributed to by the indefatigable labors of the professor whom all so honored, whose character was made up of the rocks of a solid granite. The benediction was then pronounced by the Rev. Prof. Arthur J. Mason, of the Church of England, who has been delivering the Bishop Paddock lectures in the General Theological Seminary, in New York. The public exercises of the "Jubilee" thus concluded were followed by a reception at the residence of Dr. Green. It was an inspiring day, a memorable occasion. And in order that the interest then displayed may not wholly evaporate in sentiment and speech-making, the Board of Trustees of the Seminary, as announced by Dean Murray, have, with the concurrence of the Board of Directors, resolved to make an effort to raise the sum of $100,000 toward a William Henry Green Memorial Professorship of Semitic Languages, in favor of which project, said the Dean, the addresses of the day had all been but so many solid arguments.

Note from The New York Observer of May 14, 1896.

A correspondent well says of last week's memorable jubilee at Princeton : " There was a grandeur and deep significance attached to the semi-centennial of Professor Green, of Princeton Theological Seminary, which render it a unique celebration. Other commemorations of a half century spent in a professorial chair have been connected with literature, science, or theology ; this was restricted to the Bible. The conviction deepened, as the grand addresses one after the other were delivered, that these most sincere encomiums, so well deserved, derived really their inmost significance from the fact that Dr. Green had devoted himself for fifty years to the study and exposition of the Old Testament. And this conviction was wrought into enthusiasm, as more and more the thought possessed every heart, that at this particular juncture, when the Old Testament is sorely assailed by the destructive higher criticism, Dr. Green is the giant defender of the integrity and genuine inspiration of the text. The attempt has been made persistently to disparage his powerful arguments by asserting that Dr. Green is the only great scholar who at all clings to the belief of the Church at large. Even if that were true, so far from depreciating his fame, it magnifies his position. For, as Rev. Dr. Booth admirably expressed it, 'he is Athanasius against the world.' That very large concourse of pastors and distinguished divines, those epistles congratulatory from theological schools of America and Europe, were expressions of the faith of the Church that the Bible is the Word of God. The occasion was great, the man was greater, but the Bible was the greatest." Like hundreds of others, our correspondent feels the inspiration which the occasion afforded, but not all who were there could sum it up so neatly.

The Independent of May 14, 1896.

A CONSERVATIVE SCHOLAR.

It is not always true that an old man is a conservative man ; and yet it is what might fairly have been expected that Professor William H. Green, the fiftieth anniversary of whose connection with Princeton is reported in another column, should be recognized as the leading conservative theologian in the United States. We use the word in its larger sense, as embracing not simply dogmatics, but all those studies which have to do with Christian faith.

Since Professor Green became an Instructor in Princeton College, fifty years ago, there has been an immense change in the attitude of the Christian public toward the study of the Scriptures, and our churches and theological seminaries have generally, to some extent, recognized and accepted the newer views. They have by no means given up the supernaturalism of their faith. They are no less earnest than of old in their acceptance of Jesus Christ as the crucified and risen Saviour; but the critical views which have been developed among German, French, and English scholars have been very widely accepted in as far as the composition and date of the Old Testament writings are concerned. Andover and New Haven, Union Seminary and Chicago University illustrate the attitude of three great denominations toward the higher criticism. It would now be impossible, however much individuals may protest, to shut out from universities, theological seminaries, and churches those who accept the composite and late authorship of the Pentateuch.

But to all this new drift Professor Green has presented a constant and stiff resistance. He is the incarnation of the best spirit of the old scholarship; in fact, he is a conservative Hebrew scholar, pure and simple, and such is his record. We doubt if his associates from boyhood really know him in any other relation. But he is, as we have said, the best type of such a scholar—honest, fair, clear-headed, just such an opponent as a partisan would not like to meet. It is hardly true that he is alone in his theological attitude. His position, we suppose, is very much that of Howard Osgood, the Professor of Old Testament Exegesis at Rochester Seminary, and about that of the late Professor Bissell. Some of our theological seminaries, like Princeton and McCormick, give no hospitality to the new criticism.

Professor Green has just now the pleasure of seeing a certain reaction among scholars at home and abroad against the extreme views of the critics whom he has so ably controverted. There is a tendency not so much to refer the Pentateuch to the time of Moses, but to carry back its material to a considerably earlier period, and to recognize a literary culture which existed in Palestine and the neighboring countries in the times of Moses, such as would allow a literary tradition and the preservation of documents and books. At the same time we are beginning to learn that the faith of Christianity does not depend upon one view or the other which is in dispute among the critics; and various views are held by those who are most devoted in their allegiance to the Christian faith. If it is true that progress must be made by radicals, it is also true that it is the conservatives who prevent them from making a wreck of sound scholarship; and no man in this country has done a more worthy and noble service in this line than Professor Green during the fifty years since he became a teacher at Princeton. During this time he has made the most conservative views not only respectable, but honored, by the intelligent way in which he has defended them; and if he has made the path of the higher critics hard, he has done it with such courtesy and such strength as always to retain their respect. Sound scholarship owes him a large debt; and Princeton

Seminary and the multitude of friends who were called last week to Princeton have given Professor Green no higher honor than he has justly earned.

The Presbyterian and Reformed Review, July, 1896.

THE JUBILEE OF PROFESSOR WILLIAM HENRY GREEN.

The intimate relations between Dr. Green and the editors of this *Review*, his frequent contributions to its pages, and the exceptional value of his services to theological science make it especially appropriate that we add our voice to the chorus of congratulations which have lately been tendered him upon his long and eminent career as a Teacher in Princeton Seminary. The authorities of the Seminary, as early as the autumn of 1895, determined upon this commemoration, and resolved that it be held in connection with the eighty-fourth commencement of the Institution, on May 5th following. The particular event celebrated was the accession of Dr. Green to the Seminary's Faculty of Instruction, as Tutor in Hebrew, in 1846. Mr. Green, at that time, had just attained his majority, and already had not only been graduated at both Lafayette College and Princeton Seminary, but had also spent three years as Instructor in the former Institution. With the exception of two years, during which he was the pastor of the Central Presbyterian Church of Philadelphia, Princeton has since then been his home, and he has been one of the Faculty of the Seminary. Since 1851 he has occupied the chair of Oriental and Old Testament Literature. His services to the Seminary, as teacher and administrator, have continued longer than those of any other professor, except the late Dr. Charles Hodge, and it is the unanimous judgment of the friends of the institution that in his own department they have been as valuable as those of any of his distinguished predecessors. He brought to the work to which he was called the highest ideal, and he has striven, with a lofty character and sensitive conscientiousness and exceptional gifts, to realize it in his labors in the lecture-room. At the close of a half-century he is known as one of the most illustrious teachers of the Semitic languages and Old Testament criticism and exegesis the century has given to the world. His literary product has been large and valuable, and has embraced a wide range of themes, though largely confined, of course, within the limits of the general subject indicated in the title of his chair. Though not seeking recognition as a man of affairs, he has been so valuable as a counsellor as to have occupied positions like the Chairmanship of the Old Testament Committee of the American Bible Revision Commission, and the Moderatorship of the General Assembly of the Presbyterian Church, and to have been invited by the unanimous and cordial vote of its Trustees to the Presidency of Princeton College.

APPENDIX

May 5th, on which the celebration was held, gave all that could have been desired in temperature and sunshine to the purposes of this high academic function. The regular and special trains brought to Princeton an exceptionally large number of the Alumni of the Seminary, the Moderator of the General Assembly of the Presbyterian Church, the survivors of the distinguished scholars who had been his colleagues on the Biblical Revision Committee, and many eminent men as representatives of universities and theological seminaries. A large number of letters were received from institutions of learning and individuals alike, conveying to Dr. Green not only their congratulations on the happy completion of so long a term of labor, but also their appreciation of the exceptional importance of the work which Dr. Green has accomplished.

. . . .

The addresses were singularly felicitous, and separately and as a whole were a noble tribute to the high character and distinguished career of a great scholar, teacher, and divine. Any attempt to give an account of their contents here is superseded by the intention of the Trustees of the Seminary to publish them in full. When the volume appears we hope to recur to the subject. Meanwhile we content ourselves with expressing our own feelings of gratitude to Almighty God for so prolonging the life of His servant that he has been able to see in the manifestations of this day some of the fruit of his strenuous labors, tireless devotion, and steadfast loyalty to God and the truth. The times in which his lot has been cast have been marked by much doubt and defection, and it has been his part to stand sometimes almost alone among scholars in his own department for what he deemed essential truth. His praise is that, amid all the turmoil of such a period,

>   Unmoved,
> Unshaken, unseduc'd, unterrify'd,
> His loyalty he kept, his love, his zeal ;
> Nor number, nor example with him wrought
> To swerve from truth, or change his constant mind
> Though single.

BIBLIOGRAPHY

PREPARED BY

REV. JOSEPH H. DULLES,

Librarian of Princeton Theological Seminary.

A LIST OF THE PUBLISHED WRITINGS OF PROFESSOR WILLIAM HENRY GREEN, D.D., LL.D., OF PRINCETON THEOLOGICAL SEMINARY.

The following list is arranged chronologically; the bound volumes are indicated by CAPITALS, and the periodicals in which the various articles appear by *italics*. At the close are placed Dr. Green's expositions of the International Sunday School Lessons, as these appeared in *The Sunday School Times*.

The Abundance of the Sea : a sermon preached on the 13th of November, 1850, at the ordination of the Rev. Thomas H. Newton, Chaplain of the American Seamen's Friend Society. Philadelphia, 1850, 22 pp., 8vo, paper.

Keil on Joshua. *Biblical Repertory and Princeton Review;* vol. 22 (1850), pp. 59–87.

—— The same. Reprinted in *The British and Foreign Evangelical Review*, vol. 1 (1852), pp. 380–404.

Our National Union : a sermon preached on Thanksgiving Day, December 12, 1850. Philadelphia, 1850, 26 pp., 8vo, paper.

—— The same. Bound with The Abundance of the Sea ; pp. 23–48. See above.

Inaugural Discourse. Delivered at Princeton, September 30, 1851, before the Board of Directors of the Seminary [on becoming Professor of Biblical and Oriental Literature]. Philadelphia, 1851, pp. 37–71 [of Discourses, etc.], 8vo, paper.

Delitzsch on Habakkuk. *Biblical Repertory and Princeton Review;* vol. 23 (1851), pp. 67–94.

—— The same. Reprinted in *The British and Foreign Evangelical Review;* vol. 2 (1853), pp. 590–612.

Kurtz on the Old Covenant. *Biblical Repertory and Princeton Review;* vol. 23 (1851), pp. 451-486.
——— The same. Reprinted in *The British and Foreign Evangelical Review;* vol. 2 (1853), pp. 129-159.
The Prophet Obadiah, expounded by C. P. Caspari. *Biblical Repertory and Princeton Review;* vol. 24 (1852), pp. 226-240.
——— The same. Reprinted in *The British and Foreign Evangelical Review;* vol. 2 (1853), pp. 399-411.
The Jews at K'ai-fung-foo. *Biblical Repertory and Princeton Review;* vol. 24 (1852), pp. 240-250.
The Destiny of Man : An oration delivered before the Alumni of Lafayette College, July 26, 1853. Philadelphia, 1853, 24 pp., 8vo, paper.
Theology of the Old Testament. *Biblical Repertory and Princeton Review;* vol. 25 (1853), pp. 102-120.
——— The same. Reprinted in *The British and Foreign Evangelical Review;* vol. 2 (1853), pp. 383-399.
The Religious Significance of Numbers. *Biblical Repertory and Princeton Review;* vol. 25 (1853), pp. 203-227.
——— The same. Reprinted in *The British and Foreign Evangelical Review;* vol. 4 (1855), pp. 443-463.
Recent Commentaries on the Song of Solomon. *Biblical Repertory and Princeton Review;* vol. 26 (1854), pp. 1-32.
——— The same. Reprinted in *The British and Foreign Evangelical Review;* vol. 3 (1854), pp. 221-247.
Ebrard on the Apocalypse. *Biblical Repertory and Princeton Review;* vol. 26 (1854), pp. 276-299.
——— The same. Reprinted in *The British and Foreign Evangelical Review;* vol. 4 (1855), pp. 360-380.
Origin of Writing. *Biblical Repertory and Princeton Review;* vol. 26 (1854), pp. 624-647.
Nahum's Prophecy Concerning Nineveh. *Biblical Repertory and Princeton Review;* vol. 27 (1855), pp. 102-132.
——— The same. Reprinted in *The British and Foreign Evangelical Review;* vol. 4 (1855), pp. 501-526.
Jewish Expositions of Malachi. *Biblical Repertory and Princeton Review;* vol. 27 (1855), pp. 308-327.
Monuments of the Umbrian Language. *Biblical Repertory and Princeton Review;* vol. 27 (1855), pp. 620-625.
Demotic Grammar. *Biblical Repertory and Princeton Review;* vol. 27 (1855), pp. 649-655.
Lepsius and Brugsch's Travels in Egypt. *Biblical Repertory and Princeton Review;* vol. 27 (1855), pp. 655-680.
Comparative Accentual System of the Sanscrit and Greek. *Biblical Repertory and Princeton Review;* vol. 27 (1855), pp. 680-687.

Kurtz's History of the Old Testament. *Biblical Repertory and Princeton Review ;* vol. 28 (1856), pp. 173-208.

—— The same. Reprinted in *The British and Foreign Evangelical Review ;* vol. 5 (1856), pp. 809-838.

The Money of the Bible. *Biblical Repertory and Princeton Review ;* vol. 28 (1856), pp. 238-244.

The Sacred Writings of the Parsis. *Biblical Repertory and Princeton Review ;* vol. 28 (1856), pp. 618-641.

The Mission of Saving Mercy : a sermon delivered at Newburyport, December 30, 1856, on the occasion of the installation of the Rev. Heman R. Timlow. Newburyport, 1857, 23 pp., 8vo, paper.

Tischendorf's Travels in the East. *Biblical Repertory and Princeton Review ;* vol. 29 (1857), pp. 34-50.

Spiegel's Pehlevi Grammar. *Biblical Repertory and Princeton Review ;* vol. 29 (1857), pp. 149-153.

The Book of Job. *Biblical Repertory and Princeton Review ;* vol. 29 (1857), pp. 281-327.

—— The same Reprinted in *The British and Foreign Evangelical Review ;* vol. 6 (1857), pp. 561-600.

A New Edition of Horne's Introduction to the Scriptures. *Biblical Repertory and Princeton Review ;* vol. 29 (1857), pp. 375-391.

The Scope and Plan of the Book of Ecclesiastes. *Biblical Repertory and Princeton Review ;* vol. 29 (1857), pp. 419-440.

—— The same. Reprinted in *The British and Foreign Evangelical Review ;* vol. 7 (1858), pp. 806-823.

Albania and Its People. *Biblical Repertory and Princeton Review ;* vol. 29 (1857), pp. 699-719.

Hofmann's Prophecy and Fulfilment. *Biblical Repertory and Princeton Review ;* vol. 30 (1858), pp. 189-225.

The Book of Hosea. *Biblical Repertory and. Princeton Review ;* vol. 31 (1859), pp. 74-102.

Christology. *Biblical Repertory and Princeton Review ;* vol. 31 (1859), pp. 438-463.

The Old Testament Idea of a Prophet. *Biblical Repertory and Princeton Review ;* vol. 31 (1859), pp. 689-717.

The Text of Jeremiah. *Biblical Repertory and Princeton Review ;* vol. 32 (1860), pp. 69-89.

—— The same. Reprinted in *The British and Foreign Evangelical Review ;* vol. 9 (1860), pp. 396-413.

A Sermon preached in the University Place Church, New York, May 5, 1861, in behalf of the Board of Foreign Missions of the Presbyterian Church. New York, 1861, 16 pp., 8vo, paper.

A GRAMMAR OF THE HEBREW LANGUAGE. New York, 1861, x + 322 pp., 8vo.

A GRAMMAR OF THE HEBREW LANGUAGE. 2d edition, New York, 1862, x + 400 pp., 8vo.
—— The same. 3d edition, New York, 1872, x + 400 pp., 8vo.
—— The same. 4th edition, New York, 1886, x + 400 pp., 8vo.
—— The same. New edition, carefully revised. Part I., Orthography and Etymology. New York, 1888, viii + 256 + 23 pp., 8vo.
—— The same. Part II., Syntax, pp. 257-418. New York, 1889, 8vo.
—— The same. Carefully revised throughout and the Syntax greatly enlarged. New York, 1889, viii + 418 pp., 8vo.
The Fulfilment of Prophecy. *Biblical Repertory and Princeton Review ;* vol. 33 (1861), pp. 84-122.
—— The same. Reprinted in *The British and Foreign Evangelical Review ;* vol. 10 (1861), pp. 430-460.
The Alexandrine and Sinaitic Manuscripts. *Biblical Repertory and Princeton Review;* vol. 33 (1861), pp. 150-166.
The Matter of Prophecy. *Biblical Repertory and Princeton Review ;* vol. 34 (1862), pp. 559-578.
—— The same. Reprinted in *The British and Foreign Evangelical Review ;* vol. 12 (1863), pp. 168-183.
THE PENTATEUCH VINDICATED FROM THE ASPERSIONS OF BISHOP COLENSO. New York, 1863, vi + 195 pp., 12mo.
The Date of the Books of Chronicles. *Biblical Repertory and Princeton Review ;* vol. 35 (1863), pp. 499-520.
—— The same. Reprinted in *The British and Foreign Evangelical Review ;* vol. 12 (1863), pp. 783-801.
Davidson's Introduction to the Old Testament. *Biblical Repertory and Princeton Review ;* vol. 36 (1864), pp. 53-88.
—— The same. Reprinted in *The British and Foreign Evangelical Review ;* vol. 13 (1864), pp. 397-423.
Modern Philology. *Biblical Repertory and Princeton Review ;* vol. 36 (1864), pp. 629-652.
The Value of Physical Science in the Work of Education : an address delivered, July 25, 1865, upon laying the cornerstone of the Jenks Chemical Hall at Lafayette College. Easton, 1865, 32 pp., 8vo, paper.
The Name Jehovah. *The Evangelical Quarterly Review* [Gettysburg, Pa.] ; vol. 16 (1865), pp. 86-103.
The Structure of the Old Testament. *Biblical Repertory and Princeton Review ;* vol. 37 (1865), pp. 161-187.
Relations of India with Greece and Rome. *Biblical Repertory and Princeton Review ;* vol. 38 (1866), pp. 394-415.
Dr. Williams's New Translation of the Hebrew Prophets. *Biblical Repertory and Princeton Review ;* vol. 38 (1866), pp. 646-669.
—— The same. Reprinted in *The British and Foreign Evangelical Review ;* vol. 16 (1867), pp. 153-172.

The Position of the Book of Psalms in the Plan of the Old Testament. *Biblical Repertory and Princeton Review;* vol. 39 (1867), pp. 256–287.

The Hebrew Word Yashabh. *Biblical Repertory and Princeton Review;* vol. 39 (1867), pp. 337–365.

A Sermon in Commemoration of the Rev. John Gray, D.D., Pastor of the First Presbyterian Church in Easton, Pa. Preached February 16, 1868. New York, 1868, 24 pp., 8vo, paper.

AN ELEMENTARY HEBREW GRAMMAR WITH TABLES, Reading Exercises, and a Vocabulary. New York, 1868, viii + 58 + 26 pp., 12mo.

—— The same. Second thoroughly revised edition. New York, 1871 and 1872, viii + 194 pp., 12mo.

—— The same. New edition with corrections. New York, 1879, viii + 194 pp., 12mo.

A New Reading of an Old Monument. *Our Monthly;* vol. 1, pp. 297–302 (May, 1870).

THE SONG OF SOLOMON. By Dr. Otto Zöckler. Translated from the German with additions. New York, 1871, 135 pp., cr. 8vo. [In Schaff's American edition of Lange's Commentary on the Holy Scriptures.]

Life of the Prophet Hosea. *Our Monthly;* vol. 3, pp. 40–47 (January, 1871).

—— The same. Part II. *Our Monthly;* vol. 3, pp. 139–145 (February, 1871).

Recent Expositions of Daniel. [By O. Zöckler, F. Keil, and H. W. Taylor.] *Biblical Repertory and Princeton Review;* vol. 43, pp. 397–424 (July, 1871).

A HEBREW CHRESTOMATHY; or, Lessons in Reading and Writing Hebrew. New York, 1872, viii + 261 pp., 8vo.

Assyrian Cuneiform Inscriptions. *The Presbyterian Quarterly and Princeton Review.* New series; vol. 1, pp. 516–537 (July, 1872).

The Persian Cuneiform Inscriptions the Key to the Assyrian. *The Presbyterian Quarterly and Princeton Review.* New series; vol. 2, pp. 274–292 (April, 1873).

THE ARGUMENT OF THE BOOK OF JOB UNFOLDED. New York, 1874, 369 pp., 12mo.

Assyrian Monuments and the Bible. *The Presbyterian Quarterly and Princeton Review.* New series; vol. 3, pp. 389–413 (July, 1874).

Bible History. In Preparing to Teach, pp. 103–147, Philadelphia [1875], 12mo.

Geography of the Bible. In Preparing to Teach, pp. 149–183. See above.

Archæology of the Bible. In Preparing to Teach, pp. 185–210. See above.

The Study of the Hebrew Language. *The Presbyterian Quarterly and Princeton Review.* New series; vol. 5, pp. 40–55 (January, 1876).

The Perpetual Authority of the Old Testament. *The Presbyterian Quarterly and Princeton Review.* New series; vol. 6, pp. 221–255 (April, 1877).

The Place of Samuel in Hebrew Literature. *The Library Table;* October 11, 1877, pp. 199–200.

Genuineness of the Pentateuch. *The Princeton Review;* Fifty-fourth year, pp. 143–149 (January, 1878).

Isaiah, not Pseudo-Isaiah. *The Family Treasury;* Part II. (November, 1878), pp. 648–655.

Hebrew Philology and Biblical Science. In Anglo-American Bible Revision; pp. 60–71. New York, 1879, 12mo.

Not Mythe but History. The Assyrian Monuments confirming the Books of Moses. *The Examiner and Chronicle;* April 24, 1879.

Review of W. R. Burgess's Notes, Chiefly Critical and Philological, on the Hebrew Psalms. *The Presbyterian Review;* vol. 1, p. 372 (April, 1880).

Review of Anton Scholz's Commentar zum Büche des Propheten Jeremias. *The Presbyterian Review;* vol. 1, pp. 573–574 (July, 1880).

Review of K. A. R. Töttermann's Die Weissagungen Hoseas, bis zur ersten assyrischen Deportation. *The Presbyterian Review;* vol. 1, pp. 575–576 (July, 1880).

Review of J. G. Murphy's The Books of Chronicles. *The Presbyterian Review;* vol. 1, p. 748 (October, 1880).

Review of W. Nowack's Der Prophet Hosea. *The Presbyterian Review;* vol. 1, pp. 748–750 (October, 1880).

Sermon on Romans 1:15–16. In the Quarter-century Anniversary of the Organization of the West Spruce Street Presbyterian Church of Philadelphia, pp. 79–91. Philadelphia, 1881, 8vo.

Review of J. C. K. von Hofmann's Biblische Hermeneutik. *The Presbyterian Review;* vol. 2, pp. 178–181 (January, 1881).

Review of William Imbrie's Handbook of English-Japanese Etymology. *The Presbyterian Review;* vol. 2, p. 222 (January, 1881).

Review of G. L. Studer's Der Pessimismus in Kampf mit der Orthodoxie. *The Presbyterian Review;* vol. 2, p. 597 (July, 1881).

Review of W. Robertson Smith's The Old Testament in the Jewish Church. *The Presbyterian Review;* vol. 2, pp. 780–784 (October, 1881).

Professor Robertson Smith on the Pentateuch. *The Presbyterian Review;* vol. 3, pp. 108–156 (January, 1882).

―――The same. Reprinted in *The British and Foreign Evangelical Review;* vol. 31 (1872), pp. 313–369.

Review of Robert Watts's The Newer Criticism and the Analogy of the Faith. *The Presbyterian Review;* vol. 3, pp. 411–412 (April, 1882).

Review of R. P. Stebbins's A Study of the Pentateuch for Popular Reading. *The Presbyterian Review;* vol. 3, pp. 412-413 (April, 1882).
Review of Franz Delitzsch's Old Testament History of Redemption. Translated by S. I. Curtiss. *The Presbyterian Review;* vol. 3, p. 610 (July, 1882).
Review of W. Robertson Smith's The Prophets of Israel and Their Place in History, to the Close of the Eighth Century B.C. *The Presbyterian Review;* vol. 3, pp. 769-771 (October, 1882).
MOSES AND THE PROPHETS : The Old Testament in the Jewish Church, by Professor W. Robertson Smith ; The Prophets and Prophecy in Israel, by A. Kuenen ; and the Prophets of Israel, by W. Robertson Smith, reviewed. New York, 1883, 369 pp., 12mo.
Was Moses the Author of the Pentateuch ? A supplement to H. L. Strack's article, Pentateuch, in the Schaff-Herzog Encyclopædia of Religious Knowledge. New York, 1883 and 1891, cr. 8vo.
Review of C. J. Bredenkamp's Gesetz und Propheten. *The Presbyterian Review;* vol. 4, pp. 166-168 (January, 1883).
Review of H. L. Strack's Pirke Aboth. *The Presbyterian Review;* vol. 4, p. 168 (January, 1883).
Dr. W. Robertson Smith on the Prophets of Israel. *The British and Foreign Evangelical Review;* vol. 32, pp. 201-260 (April, 1883). [Reprinted from Moses and the Prophets. New York, 1883. See above.]
Review of A. H. Charteris's The New Testament Scriptures : Their Claims, History, and Authority. *The Presbyterian Review;* vol. 4, p. 437 (April, 1883).
Introduction to the Book of Joshua. *The Sunday School Times;* June 16, 1883.
Review of Old Testament Revision: a Hand-book for English Readers. *The Independent;* June 21, 1883.
Review of Eduard Böhl's Zum Gesetz und zum Zeugniss. *The Presbyterian Review;* vol. 4, pp. 642-643 (July, 1883).
Review of S. H. Kellogg's The Jews ; or, Prediction and Fulfilment. *The Presbyterian Review;* vol. 4, pp. 650-652 (July, 1883).
Review of James Sime's The Kingdom of All-Israel : its History, Literature, and Worship. *The Presbyterian Review;* vol. 4, pp. 853-856 (October, 1883).
The Unity of I. Samuel 16-18. *The Sunday School Times;* November 17, 1883.
INTRODUCCION HISTORICA Y CRITICA AL ESTUDIO DEL ANTIGUO TESTAMENTO. Siendo las conferencias de W. H. Green, D.D. Traducidas y aumentadas por H. C. Thompson. St. Louis, 1884, xvi + 348 + liv. pp., 8vo.
The Ark Brought to Zion. *The Sunday School Times;* June 28, 1884.

THE HEBREW FEASTS, in their relation to recent critical hypotheses concerning the Pentateuch. [The Newton Lectures for 1885.] New York [1885], 329 pp., 12mo.
A Mistake to exclude the Old Testament from the Sunday School. *The Old Testament Student;* vol. 4, pp. 300–301 (March, 1885).
Review of Nathanael. Zeitschrift der Berliner Gesellschaft zur Beförderung des Christenthums unter den Juden. Edited by H. L. Strack. First year, Nos. 1–3. *The Presbyterian Review;* vol. 6, p. 330 (April, 1885).
The Septuagint and Jeroboam. *The Sunday School Times;* June 20, 1885.
Review of Charles Elliott's A Vindication of the Mosaic Authorship of the Pentateuch. *The Presbyterian Review;* vol. 5, p. 546 (July, 1885).
A Reply to Dr. Briggs on the Revised Version of the Old Testament. *The Evangelist;* July 23, 1885.
The Finding of the Law. *The Sunday School Times;* December 12, 1885.
Review of H. Clay Trumbull's The Blood Covenant : a Primitive Rite and its Bearing on Scripture. *The Presbyterian Review;* vol. 7, pp. 170–171 (January, 1886).
The Critics of the Revised Version of the Old Testament. *The Presbyterian Review;* vol. 7, pp. 304–354 (April, 1886).
Review of W. L. Pearson's The Prophecy of Joel : its Unity, its Aim, and the Age of its Composition. *The Presbyterian Review;* vol. 7, p. 381 (April, 1886).
Hosea 8:12 and its Testimony to the Pentateuch. *The Presbyterian Review;* vol. 7, pp. 585–608 (October, 1886).
Review of E. T. Bartlett and J. P. Peters's Scriptures, Hebrew and Christian. Vol. I. *The Presbyterian Review;* vol. 7, pp. 747–748 (October, 1886).
The Alleged Composite Character of Exodus I. and II. *Hebraica;* vol. 3, pp. 1–12 (October, 1886).
Critical Analysis of the Pentateuch. *The Sunday School Times;* December 25, 1886.
Review of A. Kuenen's An Historico-Critical Inquiry into the Origin and Composition of the Hexateuch. Translated by P. H. Wicksteed. *The Presbyterian Review;* vol. 8, pp. 137–147 (January, 1887).
Is the current critical Division of the Pentateuch inimical to the Christian Faith ? *The Old Testament Student;* vol. 6, pp. 315–318 (June, 1887).
Pentateuch Criticism. *The Sunday School Times;* June 18, 1887.
Review of A. H. Kellogg's Abraham, Joseph, and Moses in Egypt. *The Presbyterian Review;* vol. 8, p. 750 (October, 1887).
Mighty in the Scriptures : a sermon preached in the Chapel of the Theological Seminary, Princeton, September 18, 1887. *The Treasury;* vol. 5, pp. 463–475 (December, 1887).

Pentateuchal Analysis. No. 4 of Essays on Pentateuchal Criticism by various writers; pp. 103-137. New York, 1888, 12mo, paper.
—— The same. Reprinted in Moses and his recent Critics. Edited by Talbot W. Chambers; pp. 101-137. New York, 1889, 12mo.
Review of Victor Ryssel's Untersuchungen über die Textgestalt und die Echtheit des Buches Micha. *The Presbyterian Review;* vol. 9, pp. 140-141 (January, 1888).
Review of Franz Delitzsch's Neuer Commentar über die Genesis. *The Presbyterian Review;* vol. 9, pp. 310-314 (April, 1888).
Renan's People of Israel. *The Independent;* April 26, 1888.
Shall the analyzed Pentateuch be published in The Old Testament Student? *The Old Testament Student;* vol. 7, p. 315 (June, 1888).
The Quarter's Outlook. *The Sunday School Times;* June 16, 1888.
Semitic Study in the Theological Seminary. *Hebraica;* vol. 5, pp. 89-90 (October, 1888).
The Pentateuchal Question. *Hebraica;* vol. 5, pp. 137-189 (January, 1889).
—— The same. *Hebraica;* vol. 6, pp. 109-138; 161-211 (January and April, 1890).
—— The same. *Hebraica;* vol. 7, pp. 1-38; 104-142 (October, 1890 and January, 1891).
—— The same. *Hebraica;* vol. 8, pp. 15-64; 174-243 (October, 1891 and July, 1892).
Address at the Funeral of Rev. Alexander Taggart McGill, D.D., LL.D., in Princeton, January 16, 1889, 16 pp., 8vo, paper.
The Mosaic Origin of the Pentateuch. [Summary of an address delivered at Wellesley College, May 17, 1889.] *The Princeton College Bulletin;* vol. 1, pp. 81-82 (June, 1889).
Review of Friedrich Baethgen's Der Gott Israels und die Götter der Heiden. *The Presbyterian Review;* vol. 10, pp. 488-490 (July, 1889).
Review of E. T. Bartlett and J. P. Peters's Scriptures, Hebrew and Christian. Vol. II. *The Presbyterian Review;* vol. 10, pp. 658-659 (October, 1889).
Review of Eduard Riehm's Einleitung in das Alte Testament. Erster Theil: Die Thorah und die vorderen Propheten. *The Presbyterian and Reformed Review;* vol. 1, pp. 119-122 (January, 1890).
Primeval Chronology. *The Bibliotheca Sacra;* vol. 47, pp. 285-303 (April, 1890).
A Discourse commemorative of James Clement Moffat, D.D., June 7, 1890. 26 pp., 16mo, paper.
The Titles of the Psalms. *The Methodist Review;* vol. 72 (fifth series, vol. 6), pp. 489-506 (July, 1890).
Christian Manliness. *The Homiletic Review;* vol. 20, pp. 49-51 (July, 1890).
The Titles of the Psalms. *The Old and New Testament Student;* vol. 11, pp. 153-167 (September, 1890).

Review of W. Robertson Smith's Lectures on the Religion of the Semites. First series. The Fundamental Institutions. *The Presbyterian and Reformed Review ;* vol. 1, pp. 671-675 (October, 1890).
Review of William Wright's Lectures on the Comparative Grammar of the Semitic Languages. *The Presbyterian and Reformed Review ;* vol. 2, pp. 174-175 (January, 1891).
Dr. Briggs's Inaugural Address. *New York Observer ;* April 16, 1891.
The Bible true from the Beginning. *The Sunday School Times ;* April 24, 1891.
The Unity of Genesis : I. and II. Chapters. *The Christian Union ;* May 9, 1891.
—— The same. Reprinted in *The Treasury ;* vol. 9, pp. 230-233 (August, 1891).
—— The same. Reprinted in Timely Topics, Political, Biblical, Ethical, Practical ; pp. 275-282. New York, 1892, 12mo.
Pre-Abrahamic Chronology. *The Independent ;* July 18, 1891.
Review of Carl Hesedamm's Der Römerbrief beurtheilt und geviertheilt ; and of E. D. McRealsham's Romans Dissected. *The Presbyterian and Reformed Review ;* vol. 2, pp. 679-680 (October, 1891).
The Preacher's Mission. [Abstract from an address to a graduating class.] *The Treasury ;* vol. 9, p. 456 (November, 1891).
Not Biblical, but Anti-Biblical Criticism. *The Watchman* (Boston) ; January 14, 1892.
The Higher Criticism : a Sermon. *The Independent ;* January 28, 1892.
—— The same. Reprinted in *The Magazine of Christian Literature ;* vol. 5, pp. 475-483.
The Anti-Biblical Phase of Higher Criticism. *The Treasury ;* vol. 9, pp. 659-673 (March, 1892).
Genuineness of Isaiah XL.-LXVI. *The Presbyterian and Reformed Review ;* vol. 3, pp. 229-245 (April, 1892).
Review of S. R. Driver's An Introduction to the Literature of the Old Testament. *The Presbyterian and Reformed Review ;* vol. 3, pp. 340-344 (April, 1892).
Sermon, as retiring Moderator of the Presbyterian General Assembly, on Isaiah 45:15, " Verily thou art a God that hidest thyself, O God of Israel, the Saviour." *The Presbyterian Banner ;* May 25, 1892. [Reprinted, also, more or less fully in other religious weeklies of the same date.]
The Anti-Biblical Higher Criticism. *The Presbyterian Quarterly ;* vol. 6, pp. 341-359 (July, 1892). [An address delivered in New York, revised and enlarged.]
Christ's Desire for His People. In Princeton Sermons chiefly by the Professors of Princeton Theological Seminary ; pp. 1-28. New York and Chicago [1893], 12mo.

Christian Manliness. In Princeton Sermons ; pp. 235-259. See above.
Heresy Hunters. *The Presbyterian ;* February 15, 1893.
Liberty in the Presbyterian Church. *The Independent ;* February 23, 1893.
Review of Charles A. Briggs's The Higher Criticism of the Hexateuch. *The Presbyterian and Reformed Review ;* vol. 4, pp. 307-312 (April, 1893).
"The Story of the Spies" once more. *The Biblical World ;* vol. 1, pp. 328-344 (May, 1893).
Dr. Briggs's Higher Criticism of the Hexateuch. *The Presbyterian and Reformed Review ;* vol. 4, pp. 529-561 (October, 1893).
———— Abstract of the same. *The Princeton College Bulletin ;* vol. 6, pp. 12-13 (January, 1894).
DIE FESTE DER HEBRAER in ihrer Beziehung auf die modernen kritischen Hypothesen über den Pentateuch. Aus dem Englisch übersetzt von Otto Becher. Gütersloh, 1894, pp. viii + 304, 8vo.
The Unity of the Pentateuch. In Anti-Higher Criticism or Testimony to the Infallibility of the Bible. Edited by L. W. Munhall ; pp. 26-70. New York, 1894, 8vo.
Mosaic Origin of the Pentateuch. In Anti-Higher Criticism, etc., pp. 71-95. See above.
Critical Views Respecting the Mosaic Tabernacle. *The Presbyterian and Reformed Review ;* vol. 5, pp. 69-88 (January, 1894).
Review of C. Siegfried's The Book of Job. Critical Edition of the Hebrew Text with Notes. *The Presbyterian and Reformed Review ;* vol. 5, pp. 117-118 (January, 1894).
Review of C. M. Mead's Christ and Criticism. *The Presbyterian and Reformed Review ;* vol. 5, pp. 168-169 (January, 1894).
Who Wrote Genesis ? *The Presbyterian Journal ;* March 22, 1894.
Klostermann on the Pentateuch. *The Presbyterian and Reformed Review ;* vol. 5, pp. 261-286 (April, 1894).
Review of Eduard Rupprecht's Die Anschauung der kritischen Schule Wellhausens vom Pentateuch, u. s. w. *The Presbyterian and Reformed Review ;* vol. 5, pp. 309-310 (April, 1894).
Review of Adolf Zahn's Ernste Blicke in den Wahn der modernen Kritik des Alten Testaments. *The Presbyterian and Reformed Review ;* vol. 5, p. 310 (April, 1894).
Life and Work of Moses. *The Westminster Teacher ;* vol. 22, pp. 176-179 (May, 1894).
The Higher Critic of "The Evangelist" on the Flood. *The Mid-Continent ;* May 2, 1894.
———— The same. Article II. *The Mid-Continent ;* May 9, 1894.
———— The same. Article III. *The Mid-Continent ;* May 16, 1894.
Pentateuchal Analysis a Failure. *The Independent ;* May 3, 1894.

The Critical Partition of the Narrative of the Deluge. *The Evangelist;* May 3, 1894, pp. 10–14.

The Moses of the Critics. *The Presbyterian and Reformed Review;* vol. 5, pp. 369–397 (July, 1894).

The Sons of God and the Daughters of Men. *The Presbyterian and Reformed Review;* vol. 5, pp. 654–660 (October, 1894).

Review of Friedrich Giesebrecht's Das Buch Jeremia übersetzt und erklärt; and of Max Loehr's Die Klagelieder Jeremias übersetzt und erklärt. *The Presbyterian and Reformed Review;* vol. 5, p. 700 (October, 1894).

The Books of Moses. I. The Book of Law. *The Christian Advocate* (New York); November 12, 1894.

—— The same. II. Who Wrote Deuteronomy? *The Christian Advocate;* November 29, 1894.

—— The same. III. The Laws in Exodus, Leviticus, and Numbers. *The Christian Advocate;* December 6, 1894.

—— The same. IV. The Pentateuchal History. *The Christian Advocate;* December 13, 1894.

The Unity of Isaiah. *The Christian Advocate;* December 20, 1894.

The Book of Daniel. *The Christian Advocate;* December 27, 1894.

THE HIGHER CRITICISM OF THE PENTATEUCH. New York, 1895, pp. viii + 184, 8vo.

THE UNITY OF THE BOOK OF GENESIS. New York, 1895, pp. xviii + 583, 8vo.

Deism, Rationalism, and Anti-Biblical Criticism. *The Christian Advocate* (New York); January 3, 1895.

Fallacies of Higher Criticism. *The Homiletic Review;* vol. 29, pp. 99–106 (February, 1895).

Review of Eduard Rupprecht's Das Räthsel des Fünfbuches Mose und seine Lösung. *The Presbyterian and Reformed Review;* vol. 6, pp. 345–346 (April, 1895).

Review of Adolf Zahn's Ernste Blicke in der Wahn der modernen Kritik des Alten Testaments. Neue Folge. *The Presbyterian and Reformed Review;* vol. 6, p. 346 (April, 1895).

Review of R. V. French's Lex Mosaica; or, The Law of Moses and the Higher Criticism. *The Presbyterian and Reformed Review;* vol. 6, pp. 346–348 (April, 1895).

Review of Charles Jordan's Are the Books of Moses Holy Scripture? or, The Modern Theory of the Pentateuch Anti-Biblical. *The Presbyterian and Reformed Review;* vol. 6, p. 348 (April, 1895).

Review of R. B. Girdlestone's Deuterographs. *The Presbyterian and Reformed Review;* vol. 6, pp. 348–349 (April, 1895).

"The Impregnable Rock of Holy Scripture." *The Oxford* [Presbyterian Church, Philadelphia] *Journal;* December, 1895.

Review of August Dillmann's Handbuch der Alttestamentlichen Theologie. *The Presbyterian and Reformed Review;* vol. 7, pp. 543-544 (July, 1896).

Critical Notes on the International Sunday School Lessons that appeared in *The Sunday School Times*, arranged according to the books of the Bible in their order and according to the lesson quarters :

Genesis ; January-June, 1887.
Exodus ; January-June, 1881 ; April-June, 1887, and January-March, 1888.
Leviticus ; January-March, 1887, and July-September, 1888.
Numbers ; July-September, 1888.
Deuteronomy ; July-September, 1888.
Joshua ; July-September, 1883, and October-December, 1888.
Judges ; July-September, 1883, and October-December, 1888.
Ruth ; July-September, 1888, and October-December, 1888.
I. Samuel ; July-December, 1883, and July-September, 1889.
II. Samuel ; July-September, 1884, and October-December, 1889.
I. Kings ; October-December, 1884 ; October-December, 1889 ; and January-March, 1891.
II. Kings ; October-December, 1885 ; January-March, 1886 ; and January-June, 1891.
I. Chronicles ; October-December, 1884.
II. Chronicles ; April-June, 1891.
Ezra ; January-March, 1886.
Nehemiah ; January-March, 1886.
Esther ; January-March, 1886.
Psalms ; July-September, 1884 ; January-March, 1888 ; October-December, 1889 ; and April-June, 1892.
Proverbs ; October-December, 1884, and October-December, 1889.
Ecclesiastes ; October-December, 1884.
Isaiah ; October-December, 1885 ; April-June, 1890 ; January-June, 1891 ; and January-March, 1892.
Jeremiah ; January-March, 1892.
Ezekiel ; January-March, 1892.
Daniel ; January-March, 1886 ; April-September, 1890 ; and April-June, 1892.
Hosea ; April-June, 1891.
Amos ; April-June, 1891.
Jonah ; October-December, 1885, and April-June, 1891.
Malachi ; January-March, 1886.

www.ingramcontent.com/pod-product-compliance
Lightning Source LLC
Chambersburg PA
CBHW020839160426
43192CB00007B/720